SECRETS OF
GREAT COMMUNICATORS

**Simple, Powerful Strategies for Reaching the
Heart of Your Audience**

SECRETS OF
GREAT COMMUNICATORS

Simple, Powerful Strategies for Reaching the Heart of Your Audience

Jeff Myers

BROADMAN
&HOLMAN
PUBLISHERS

Nashville, Tennessee

10-digit ISBN: 0805468803
13-digit ISBN: 9780805468809

Published by Broadman & Holman Publishers
Nashville, Tennessee

DEWEY: 920
SUBHD: COMMUNICATORS-BIOGRAPHY / COMMUNICATION

Scripture text is from The Holy Bible, *Holman Christian Standard Bible* ®, Copyright © 1999, 2000, 2001, 2002, 2003 by Holman Bible Publishers. Other "Credits, Permissions, and Sources" are listed at the back of the book.

1 2 3 4 5   10   09   08   07   06

ACKNOWLEDGMENTS

Special thanks to:

My wife, Danielle, and my children.
The Myers Institute team for the dogged pursuit of a compelling idea.
The Summit Ministries team, especially Todd Cothran, Joel Putnam, and Kevin Bywater
for making my video coaching possible.
Bryan College, whose strategic partnership gives me the freedom and flexibility
to pursue my calling.
David Austin, Chris Jeub, Meleah Smith, and Regina Thorpe, who edited this volume
(if any participles yet dangle, or any incorrect spellings remain, the fault is mine alone).
Alan Toliver, my assistant in the early days of this project, who held things together during
the months of absence necessary to complete this volume.
Ramon Williamson: for your persistent, perspicacious coaching—I'm finally starting to get it.

CONTENTS

Focus on Great Communicators:
Winston Churchill

23

Notes
Video Session Five

— CHAPTER FIVE —

Deliver Your Talk with Confidence

Focus on Great Communicators:
Patrick Henry

— APPENDIX ONE—

Speech Outlines for Every Occasion

141

Speech Outlines

149

SECRETS OF
GREAT COMMUNICATORS

Simple, Powerful Strategies for Reaching the Heart of Your Audience

Are You Ready for a World-Changing Experience?

> KEY QUOTE:
> If you can conquer your fear of public speaking
> and communicating with other people,
> there is almost no limit to the impact you can have
> on the world around you.
> —Jeff Myers

CONGRATULATIONS ON BEGINNING YOUR STUDY of *Secrets of Great Communicators!* Public speaking is a meaningful and fulfilling part of *my* life, and I hope it will become that for *you* by the time we've worked through this course together. I love public speaking and want you to feel the same. But I also must assure you it wasn't always like that for me. When I was a child, the mere *thought* of public speaking reduced me to tears. But I conquered that fear and have found a remarkable level of confidence, joy and success in living out my God-given gifts. In addition to having delivered more than 3,500 speeches, I have coached thousands of people in mastering the skills of great communication.

This six-step video coaching system will have you making a compelling speech in just a few hours, even if the thought of speaking in public scares you to death right now. Most speech programs focus on teaching what good communication is, but in my approach, we don't have time for that. Since I intend to streamline your way to great public speaking by addressing the issues and teaching the skills that will give you a life-long pattern of making an impact on people, this system focuses on

"Men are polished, through act and speech, each by each, as pebbles are smoothed on the rolling beach."

—John Townsend Trowbridge
A Home Idyl

learning and *practicing* key speech principles. Follow the simple instructions, do the exercises, and you will be amazed at how your skills improve. By the time you reach the last chapter, you will have organized and delivered an effective speech that you could confidently give to any audience. As the life of many a famous person demonstrates, you may be just the person God is looking for, regardless of how you perceive your skills now.

Great Communication Turns Ordinary People Into World-Changers

The year: 1775. The place: St. John's Church in Richmond, Virginia.

Having suffered great misery at the hands of the British Crown, 122 Virginia colonial delegates met to determine a course of action. Patrick Henry, a 38-year-old self-taught lawyer, proposed that the colony prepare a plan for "embodying, arming, and disciplining" an army to stand against British tyranny.

As was the custom, Henry gave a speech defending his resolution. Without using notes, he delivered an eloquent address that changed the course of human history. Here's how he concluded:

> It is in vain, sir, to extenuate the matter. Gentlemen may cry, "Peace! Peace!"—but there is no peace. The war is actually begun! The next gale that sweeps from the north will bring to our ears the clash of resounding arms! Our brethren are already in the field! Why stand we here idle? What is it that gentlemen wish? What would they have? Is life so dear, or peace so sweet, as to be purchased at the price of chains and slavery? Forbid it, Almighty God! I know not what course others may take; but as for me, give me liberty, or give me death!

With Henry's electrifying words, the colony of Virginia passed the resolution, organized a militia, and began preparing for the war of independence from Great Britain.

Patrick Henry's words are among the most recognizable and revered ever uttered in a speech. Yet scholars who study the man are amazed at the sheer ordinariness of his life. He had no formal education. His family life was unremarkable. He had experienced failure in business. He wrote no great philosophical treatises, and few of his writings or speeches are preserved for us today. *Yet Patrick Henry changed the world.*

The picture that emerges from Patrick Henry's life is that of a "regular guy" who loved God, loved his family, and loved his country. And this shouldn't surprise us—*God always seems to use ordinary people to make an extraordinary difference in the world.* He uses the likes of Patrick Henry, and he uses people like *you and me.* God wants you to become confident in speaking truth. He wants you to overcome your fears and unleash your gifts. He wants you to bring a message of grace and redemption to the world around you.

As you grow as a communicator, tremendous blessings will flow into your life. You will improve your social relationships. Your career options will expand. People will treat what you say as important, and as your credibility grows, you will experience new meaning and fulfillment in life. You will be equipped to take advantage of new opportunities. You'll rest secure knowing that your life counts for something. You will have something worth living—and if need be, dying—for.

Six Steps To Communication Success

Only six steps stand between you and confident public speaking. *Secrets of Great Communicators* will show you how to master each. Through this coaching, you will:

1. See your true potential as a great communicator.

2. Conquer your fear of public speaking.

3. Be equipped to organize your talk for maximum impact.

4. Find out how to understand and persuade your audience.

> "Where thou art obliged to speak, be sure to speak the Truth: For Equivocation is half way to Lying, as Lying, the whole way to Hell."
>
> —William Penn
> (1644-1718)

> "Now Faithful play the Man, speak for thy God: Fear not the wicked's malice, nor their rod: Speak boldly man, the Truth is on thy side; Die for it, and to Life in triumph ride."
>
> —John Bunyan
> (1628-1688)
> *The Pilgrim's Progress*

> "Speech is a mirror of the soul: as a man speaks, so is he."
>
> —Publius Syrus (42 BC)

5. Learn how to effectively deliver your message to the audience.

6. Master the finer points of what makes great speakers great.

Secrets of Great Communicators also includes two beneficial appendices! The first provides you with dozens of outlines for all of the speech occasions in your life. Whether you want to introduce a guest of honor with flair or deliver a stirring eulogy for a departed loved one, you'll find the help you need right here. The second appendix recommends robust resources to help you take your speech-making ability to the next level—whether you want to use technology to "wow" an audience, develop and promote a seminar, or turn speech-making into a profitable business.

How *Secrets of Great Communicators* Works

Each step in the *Secrets of Great Communicators* system offers a five-point learning strategy that helps you discover and master each of the significant facets of speech delivery in a surprisingly short period of time. Take a moment to read through this overview so the outline for each chapter will make more sense.

Video Coaching

Since I can't actually be there with you, I'll coach you through each step in the communication development process using video programs taped with a "live" audience. By using the fill-in-the-blank outlines to record key points from each video session, you will retain 80 to 90 percent more content than by just watching. Be sure to fill in the blanks and write other comments of interest in the space provided.

Focus on a Great Communicator

I'll whet your appetite by sharing stories of ordinary people who became great communicators that had an extraordinary influence on the world. These people will inspire you and give you confidence to develop the particular skills that made them successful.

Coaching

The bulk of each chapter highlights the key points from the associated video coaching session and offers additional insights and personal encouragement as you apply each lesson to your own life.

Personal Application

Thought-provoking analysis questions draw your attention to the strategies you need to master each public speaking skill. You also will find enlightening worksheets strategically placed along the way. These tools will reveal your own communication style so that you can improve.

Speech Outline

Chapters 2, 3, 4, and 5 include speech outlines which provide you with tools to immediately apply each principle, step by step, in a way that draws out your own natural communication style. You will find instructions for writing a speech, an outline to follow in constructing your speech, and a sample speech to show how it might be done.

> "Speak gently! 'tis a little thing Dropp'd in the heart's deep well; The good, the joy, that it may bring Eternity shall tell."
>
> —Attributed to: G. W. Langford

PUBLIC SPEAKING HELPS ACHIEVE YOUR GOALS

(16 minutes)

How You Benefit from Learning the Art of Public Speaking

- You gain credibility and _____.

- You find more _____ and fulfillment.

- You become a better _____.

- You become more _____ of your gifts.

- You _____ the nature of your Creator.

Five Ways This Series Will Help You

1. Help you _____ your fear of public speaking.

2. Show you how to _____ your talk for maximum impact.

3. Give you strategies for reaching the _____ of your audience.

4. Explain how to _____ your message with confidence.

5. Reveal the secrets of an _____ speech.

CHAPTER ONE

Discover How Public Speaking Will Help You Achieve Your Highest Goals

KEY QUOTE:

God has made you in His image,
and He wants you to be a communicator
who will reflect His image to a world that so desperately needs Him.
—Jeff Myers

Focus on Great Communicators:
Ronald Reagan

CHAPTER AT A GLANCE

- The first step on a life-changng journey.
- God chooses ordinary people to accomplish the extraordinary.
- Push beyond terror and embrace boldness and creativity.
- You, too, have come to a royal position for such a time as this.
- Successful communicators are chosen to be leaders.
- When communication falters, the world suffers.
- Speak up—with confidence!
- Six ways communication skills help you reach your dreams.
- Communication excellence is great—but there is a catch.

RONALD REAGAN IS ONE OF America's most beloved former presidents. He spoke articulately and with great wit, always reflecting the thoughts and feelings of his audience. Mr. Reagan began his career as a sports announcer, an unlikely start for a future president. But a screen test led to a long-lasting career as an actor, and on the sound stages of Hollywood, Reagan honed the secret skill that would propel him to worldwide fame.

Most speakers address an audience loudly and slowly, as if talking to an unruly crowd. On television, such speakers come across as arrogant and hot-headed. Movie actors, on the other hand, learn

Words that shaped the 20th Century:

"Speak softly and carry a big stick."

"We have nothing to fear but fear itself."

"We shall never surrender!"

"I shall return!"

"Ask not what your country can do for you. Ask what you can do for your country."

"I have a dream!"

"Mr. Gorbachev, tear down this wall!"

(Who said it? Answers on page 12).

to communicate in a calm, personal and even vulnerable way. Ronald Reagan applied this communication style to politics. He did not speak *to* people; he conversed *with* them.

Reagan's ability to explain conservative principles in everyday language was cemented in a 1964 address supporting Barry Goldwater's presidential campaign. The address, "A Time for Choosing," displayed Reagan's humor and graceful oratory. Although Goldwater lost, Reagan went on to become governor of California and in 1980, President of the United States.

As president, Reagan renewed hope by declaring that it was "morning in America." In one of his most dramatic speeches, he challenged then Soviet leader Mikhail Gorbachev to tear down the wall which imprisoned East Berlin: "Mr. Gorbachev, open this gate! Mr. Gorbachev, tear down this wall." The wall soon fell, and with it toppled most of the Communist governments in Europe.

Critics dismissed him as unintellectual, but President Reagan had the last laugh. His leadership renewed the economy, ensured the demise of Communism in Europe, and transformed how Americans view the role of their government. These dramatic changes likely would not have been possible without Mr. Reagan's ability to communicate in a personable and down-to-earth manner.

The First Step on a Life-Changing Journey

Like most great communicators, Ronald Reagan did not set out to make speeches. He set out to make a difference—and his speeches reflected that passion. The first step in becoming a great communicator is to be convinced that being a better public speaker will help you make the difference God desires you to make. You've got to *want* to change. That's what Chapter One does; it opens your mind to the possibility that you, too, can learn to influence others in a powerful, positive way.

Did you know that only 5% of Americans say they would be willing to give a speech if called on to do so? That means 95% of us would refuse!

Imagine for a moment what it would be like to be among the 5% who are willing to speak publicly. These people get the best jobs. Their coworkers respect them. The boss views them as indispensable. They have influence in their church and in the community. They stand for truth at political gatherings. . . and people listen! These elite few quickly rise to the top.

So, by the end of this first step on your way to confident public speaking

• You will see how words can change the world.

• You will be convinced God has a remarkable plan for your life as a great communicator.

• You will understand how communication skills accelerate your learning and social development, allowing you to gain people's trust and expand your influence.

• You will recognize how communication skills extend your thinking skills, allowing you to think quickly on your feet.

• You will be convinced of six specific areas in which better communication skills will help you achieve your goals and realize your dreams.

It is time to break away from your fears and frustrations. It is time to *stop* thinking of public speaking as a mysterious gift and *start* seeing it as a skill *you* can master. A world of influence and fulfillment awaits you.

God Chooses Ordinary People to Accomplish the Extraordinary

The Bible tells of an ordinary girl who was given a world-changing assignment by God. Esther was kidnapped from her home and chosen as queen to the most powerful monarch in the world of that day, King Xerxes of Persia.

Shortly after the marriage, Esther's wise cousin Mordecai, one of the palace guards, discovered that the king had been tricked by his evil advisor, Haman, into sanctioning the cold-blooded murder of all of Esther's people, the Jews. Mordecai instructed Esther to do something that could cost her her life: "To approach the king, implore his favor, and plead with him personally for her people" (Esther 4:8).

This was not what Esther wanted to hear. She replied that she had not been allowed to speak to the king for over a month, and that if she went to see him unannounced, the law required her to be put to death.

Mordecai, though, was unmoved: "Don't think that you will escape the fate of all the Jews because you are in the king's palace. If you keep silent at this time, liberation and deliverance will come to the Jewish people from another place, but you and your father's house will be destroyed. Who knows, perhaps you have come to the kingdom for such a time as this" (Esther 4:13-14).

Push Beyond Terror and Embrace Boldness and Creativity

Esther must have been terrified. How could a young girl stop a plot set in motion by the most powerful man on earth? Nevertheless, Esther replied, "I will go to the king even if it is against the law. If I perish, I perish" (Esther 4:16).

Esther did go to the king, and her boldness and creativity in a time of crisis saved her people. She invited Xerxes to a special dinner which she used as an opportunity to invite him to a second dinner. The king was so pleased

> "They called it the Reagan revolution. Well, I'll accept that, but for me it always seemed more like the great rediscovery, a rediscovery of our values and our common sense."
>
> —Ronald Reagan

with this attention that he became overwhelmed with affection for Esther.

Esther's appeal to the king was respectful but shrewd. She persuaded him that Haman had usurped his authority. Then she revealed Haman's plan to kill Mordecai, the man who had once saved the king's life. Xerxes was incensed at Haman's evil scheming and ordered him to be executed on the very gallows Haman had built for Mordecai. The Jews of Persia were saved.

Little else is known about Esther. She is not mentioned by ancient historians, and some commentators believed that Vashti, the queen Esther had replaced, regained the throne. It is also interesting to note that God is not mentioned in the book of Esther. Yet His presence and guidance in the affairs of Esther and her family could not be more obvious. God chose Esther for a remarkable and often terrifying set of circumstances in order to save His people. She ascended to a royal position "for such a time as this."

You, Too, Have Come to a Royal Position For Such a Time as This

Each of us has received a call from God to step forward and unleash the gifts He has given us for the benefit of the world. As you discover the secrets to communicating boldly and persuasively, you will find yourself better equipped to push through barriers that prevent you from making your life count. In this first step of *Secrets of Great Communicators* you will learn from some of the best: Ronald Reagan, Martin Luther, and others—ordinary people who accomplished the extraordinary. It is your destiny as well.

Successful Communicators Are Chosen to Be Leaders

In 1517, a German priest and university professor challenged Catholic authorities to debate him on his questions regarding church doctrine. Rather than debate, the Pope condemned the man and directed Emperor Charles V to put him on trial for heresy.

It is hard to imagine today how suicidal it was to question the Church in that day. To be convicted of heresy and to be excommunicated was thought to revoke a person's salvation. If the Church were right, this priest would be condemned to hell. Rarely in history had anyone staked everything on the truth of Scripture—salvation by grace alone through faith.

The priest was Martin Luther whose bold challenge led to the Reformation and the establishment of Protestantism, affecting the lives of billions of people over the last 500 years.

At his trial, Luther was asked to recant the doctrine he had taught. But he countered: "I implore you by the mercies of God to prove to me by the writings of the prophets and apostles that I am in error. As soon as I shall be convinced, I will instantly retract all my errors, and will myself be the first to seize my writings and commit them to the flames. . . . Since Your Most Serene Majesty and Your High Mightinesses require of me a simple, clear, and direct answer, I will give one, and it is this: I cannot submit my faith either to the Pope or to the council, because it is as clear as noonday that they have fallen into error and even into glaring inconsistency with themselves. . . . I neither can nor will retract anything; for it cannot be right for a Christian to speak against his conscience. Here I stand; I cannot do otherwise."

Like all of history's great communicators, Luther recognized the creative power of words and knew how to reach deep into the heart of his audience. Challenging prevailing beliefs, attitudes, and values, his sermons and writings shaped the course of history. By forcing people to stop and think, Luther made the Reformation a defining moment in history.

When we look at the life of Martin Luther, we see the truth about the nature of influence: *those who communicate effectively are chosen to be leaders.*

The great communicators of history were once young people who faced decisions about the course of action they should take for their lives. In choosing to communicate with others, they chose the high road, and their influence lives on through their words.

During your life, you will face many decisions affecting not only your future, but the future of your nation. As you prepare for these challenges, effective communication will help you gain influence and make a difference. And not a moment too soon—because the world is in big trouble.

When Communication Falters, the World Suffers

We live in tough times. Political leaders up to the highest levels have become corrupt. Irresponsible national spending has burdened future generations with massive debt. Entertainment companies churn out movies and recordings that encourage the lowering of moral standards. Criminals go unpunished while innocent citizens lie awake at night in fear. The moral foundation of our nation is openly mocked in university classrooms and halls of justice.

In the chaos, people are becoming increasingly apathetic and ignorant. Educational tests are rewritten every year to accommodate the lack of knowledge. Teachers stop teaching traditional values for fear of attack by "political correctness" police.

The ability of people to communicate effectively is at an all-time low. One study demonstrates that 75% of young people couldn't even give a basic set of directions to a nearby location. Neighbors hardly know one another, and few take the time to talk to or to care about those around them.

"I refuse to exploit, for political purposes, my opponent's youth and inexperience."

—Ronald Reagan
(when questioned in the 1984 campaign about concerns over his advancing age)

"My young friends, history is a river that takes us as it will. But we have the power to navigate, to choose direction, and make our passage together. The wind is up, the tide is high, and the opportunity for a long and fruitful journey awaits us. Generations hence will honor us for having begun the voyage."

—Ronald Reagan

When the people of a nation stop communicating, they lose the common purpose that made them great. Their cities become moral ghost towns. People live aimlessly because they have no cause for which they are willing to die. The cry of the populace is, "Just leave me alone." Perhaps the ultimate hell is that the wish will be granted.

It is not unlikely that our own nation will collapse not through an explosive roar, but through a deafening silence. This silence must be broken in our generation. We may never get another chance.

Speak Up—With Confidence!

You may be saying, "I agree that we must break the silence, but how? How can Christians reach others for the kingdom in a world such as this?"

John 1:1 says, "In the beginning was the Word." The Greek word for "Word" is logos, which means "a thought expressed." God spoke the universe into existence through the person of Jesus Christ. The *mind* of God was expressed through the *Word* of God.

Is it not ironic that in the postmodern world, when the "logos" is rejected, people lose the ability to communicate deeply with each other? Don't you see this happening today?

• Rather than shopping at the corner market, people roam the aisles of "mega-stores" hardly making eye contact with others.

• Neighbors move from the front porch to the back deck, from the parlor to the TV room.

• Music becomes a means of isolating the self from others rather than drawing people together in common understanding.

• Political groups stop cooperating for the good of the nation and resort to vicious personal attacks.

• Unable to express their true feelings to loved ones, folks rely on greeting cards manufactured by professional writers of emotion.

Because God is a communicative God and because we are made in His image, we must learn to use words to create, to encourage, to build community, and to reach out to those who are isolated by the fallout of a fallen world.

Perhaps, with the Word as our model, our response to cultural decline is to break the silence by learning all over again how to express the grace that we ourselves have received from God. As we will see in the next section, expressing grace very well could be the missing ingredient in developing a deep sense of meaning and satisfaction in life.

Six Ways Communication Skills Help You Reach Your Dreams

In a complex and competitive world, people with excellent communication skills have a tremendous advantage over those without them. Most jobs—even so-called "unskilled" positions—require public speaking, and even companies hiring for jobs which focus primarily on technical skills increasingly hire candidates who possess strong communication abilities over those who do not. The Department of Labor asserts that seven out of ten jobs require good speech skills. Without clear communication, the world's systems do not operate properly and cause great hurt. So, if you are willing to unleash your gifts and communicate dynamically with the world around you, six marvelous changes will occur in your life.

1. You Will Find a Stronger Sense of Purpose.

A fear common to a great many people is that they will not discover the purpose for their existence. They give up, convinced that life is meaningless, hopeless, and boring. Your life—and mine—should not be like that. Jesus said, "I have come that they may have life and have it in abundance" (John 10:10).

Purpose emerges, in part, through action—we find our sense of purpose through trying lots of things. A person who knows how to communicate well and is willing to speak publicly will discover abundant opportunities. I have seen young people who develop communication skills start Bible studies, organize community activities, testify before legislatures, appear on television, conduct radio interviews, participate in press conferences, speak to community groups, and run political campaigns.

Through communication activities, you can develop a vision for the world around you, and ultimately for the things of God.

2. You Will Become More Aware of the World Around You

In his letter to the Philippians, the Apostle Paul calls us to "do nothing out of rivalry or conceit, but in humility to consider others as more important than yourselves" (Philippians 2:3-4). As you learn to communicate with greater impact, you become more sensitive to those around you and more aware of the significance of everyday events. Your heightened senses actually increase your intelligence and make you aware of possibilities you otherwise might never have dreamed exist, and the possibilities make the world more intriguing than ever.

3. You Will Become a Better Learner

Limited by the narrowness of their self-perceptions, unsuccessful people

> "There is a flickering spark in all of us which, if struck at just the right age, can light up the rest of our lives."
>
> —Ronald Reagan

> "Government must not supersede the will of the people or the responsibilities of the people. The function of government is not to confer happiness, but to give men the opportunity to work out happiness for themselves."
>
> —Ronald Reagan

get stuck in a rut. Successful people, on the other hand, aggressively seek out opportunities to learn, to grow, and to improve their effectiveness.

Communication skills can really help you shine. Learning to communicate well verbally strengthens both your reading and writing skills. Stronger reading and writing skills, in turn, allow you to take in more information and to make better use of it. One study of college students noted that those who display the greatest mastery of words exhibit a higher level of scholastic ability than their counterparts, regardless of their department of study. Similarly, research with children shows that those who are given the opportunity to communicate orally and who are encouraged to use language as a tool to satisfy their curiosity develop a stronger foundation of language learning which ultimately helps them become better communicators. "My language is the limit of my world," wrote philosopher Ludwig Wittgenstein. As you expand your communication ability, you will be amazed at the world of opportunities that open up to you.

4. You Will Become a Better Thinker

Have you ever found yourself in a conversation in which you did not know what to say? Have you ever thought of a retort or argument to use—three hours after the discussion was over? Good communication skills help generate structures in your mind to promote creativity. That means you

become adept at "thinking on your feet," quickly and accurately understanding a situation and formulating a response to it. Wouldn't it be great to always know the right thing to say? Wouldn't it boost your confidence if you knew you could improvise on your feet and give a great presentation? Communication skills move you down that road of self-assurance.

5. You Will Develop Greater Poise in Social Situations

People expect good communicators to know how to act in a socially appropriate manner. If your behavior is awkward and embarrassing, or if you are unsure of how to communicate your thoughts clearly, you are seen as unintelligent by your teachers and bosses. On the other hand, polished communication skills open doors throughout life. In his book *Top Performance*, Zig Ziglar reports that 85 percent of the reason a person gets a job, keeps it, and moves ahead in that job is *people skills and people knowledge!*

In my own life, I have noticed that the better I articulate my thoughts, the more people tend to view me as a leader. They take stock of what I say, and they say good things about me when I am not there. They also think of me for greater and greater opportunities. In short, they *trust* me. As your communication skills improve, you will find the same thing happening to you.

6. You Will Relate Better to Others

Communication skills connect us to our environment. People who "link-up" with their environment find it easier to relate to others and, therefore, enjoy smoother social interaction. Dozens of studies show that people who communicate well—regardless of social status and physical appearance—are more attractive to others.

"Being popular" may not be a major goal in your life. But consider this: people who are highly regarded by others are more influential. They can get people to work together. They can organize things. They can make progress toward their own goals and ultimately make life better for themselves and those around them.

Have you ever been frustrated over being unable to persuade a person of something important to you? Have you ever been discouraged at the state of things, wishing you could create change? Now is your chance to develop the skills to help you do just that.

When all six of these factors are taken together, communication training unleashes your potential and generates enthusiasm. Yet, there is a downside.

Communication Excellence is Great— But There Is a Catch

When you consider all the benefits that flow from developing good communication skills, doesn't it quicken your pulse? God has created you with incredible potential! *Secrets of Great Communicators* offers the tools you need to start traveling down the road to communication success, if you are willing.

But before we go further, a word of warning is in order. There are many things I, as your coach, cannot do for you. For instance, I cannot make you read or apply the energizing material contained in this system. You will need self-discipline and a willing mind to do that. Moreover—and this is a great concern—I cannot guide you into the proper use of your powerful new skills.

When you are armed with potent communication skills, people will begin to follow you and do what you say. They may place power in your hands. Yet you must be aware that there is danger in this power. Adolph Hitler was as great a communicator as Ronald Reagan, perhaps even better. However, he employed his communication skills to manipulate and deceive the masses. Memories of the hideous bloodshed he spawned still haunt us today.

As long as people have sought to improve their communication abilities, it has been understood that someone must *desire to do good* in order to properly apply good gifts. Anything short of proper motives is manipulation and deceit. King Solomon said it this way:

> From the fruit of his mouth a man's stomach is satisfied; he is filled with the product of his lips.

> Life and death are in the power of the tongue,

> "The American dream is not that every man must be level with every other man. The American dream is that every man must be free to become whatever God intends he should become."
>
> —Ronald Reagan

"I know that it is often difficult to stand up for one's beliefs when they are being harshly challenged. But as one who has seen many challenges over a long lifetime, I can assure you that personal faith and conviction are strengthened, not weakened, in adversity."

—Ronald Reagan

and those who love it will eat its fruit. (Proverbs 18:20-21)

It is true that we live in difficult times. Yet, difficult times can bring out the best in those whose hearts are committed to God. The Apostle Peter declared, "But you are a chosen race, a royal priesthood, a holy nation, a people for His possession, so that you may proclaim the praises of the One who called you out of darkness into His marvelous light" (I Peter 2:9). Yes, you too have come to a royal position "for such a time as this." Your investment in improving your ability to communicate will expand your capacity to shape events and influence the world toward truth and righteousness.

Before you go on to Chapter Two, take a few moments to journal your responses to the seven thought-provoking questions in the following pages. They will help cement these lessons in your mind and build a stronger foundation for the succeeding steps.

Personal Application

Take a few minutes, and jot down answers to these questions. They will help you think through your personal challenges as you begin improving your public speaking skills.

- What specific qualities make someone a great communicator?

- Why do you think most people are so afraid of public speaking?

WHAT IS PSYCHOLOGICAL NOISE?

Every public speaker knows what noise is. A cell phone ringing, a siren, or crashing dishes can break the attention of an audience and destroy the most dramatic moment of a speech. Psychological noise—distraction or "noise" in the mind of an audience—does the same thing.

Exhaustion, sadness, uncertainty, a feeling of being overwhelmed—all of these shut down an audience's ability to listen to and apply what a speaker says.

Successful speech-givers learn to arrange the environment (temperature, light, sound quality) to make it easier for the audience to listen. They also become adept at identifying with the feelings of the audience and focusing its attention on the issue at hand.

• What are some examples of "psychological noise" that have hindered you from listening to a speaker in the past?

• In what areas of life could public speaking help you develop your gifts and talents?

• Look in the concordance of your Bible, and write down three Scripture references related to speaking, the use of the tongue, or how words are used. What do these verses say about the proper use of communication skills?

• Write down the names of two people (besides the ones listed in this chapter) who use or have used their communication ability to influence the world. What did they achieve, and how did their communication skills help?

• What are some problems or issues in our society about which you might be motivated to speak out?

CONQUER YOUR FEAR OF PUBLIC SPEAKING

(20 minutes)

Six steps to conquering public speaking anxiety:

1. Identify the _____ of anxiety.

2. Explain your fears in a _____ way.

3. Focus on the _____, not yourself.

4. Invest time in _____.

5. Speak only on the _____ you _____ about.

6. Develop a sense of _____.

CHAPTER TWO

Conquer Your Fear of Public Speaking

KEY QUOTE:

How can you really overcome your fear of people in an audience? You can love them. You can take their concerns as your concerns.
—Jeff Myers

Focus on Great Communicators:
Winston Churchill

CHAPTER AT A GLANCE

- Attacking fear leads to top performance.
- Fearful? You're not the first!
- A world of purpose, influence, opportunity, and excitement awaits you.
- What sets courageous people apart?
- Public speaking isn't the only communication style.
- Discover the source of your apprehension.
- Use your communication strengths to compensate for your weaknesses.
- Build rapport by addressing your fears.
- The best fear-conquering strategy of all.
- Three steps to take right now.

UPON ASSUMING THE POSITION OF Prime Minister of Great Britain during World War II, Winston Churchill announced, "I have nothing to offer but blood, toil, tears, and sweat." It was, in one sentence, a summary of his approach to all of life. Short in stature, weak as a child, unloved by his parents, and plagued by a speech impediment, Churchill's rise to prominence was miraculous. Many times fear overwhelmed him. Once he even broke down midway through a speech to the House of Commons. He lost often and had many enemies. Yet he pressed on.

Nervous? So was the Apostle Paul! He knew he didn't measure up to standards of flowery oratory (see 2 Corinthians 10:10). Yet he prayed for strength and admonished others to be strong as well:

"Your speech should always be gracious, seasoned with salt, so that you may know how you should answer each person."
—Colossians 4:6

"I am able to do all things through Him who strengthens me."
—Philippians 4:13

"For when I am weak, then I am strong."
—2 Corinthians 12:10b

In addition to giving countless speeches, Churchill authored 50 books and hundreds of articles. Stephen Mansfield writes, "His love affair with words and their meaning was the very lifeblood of his powerful kind of leadership."

When it came to speech-writing, Churchill left nothing to chance. He wrote every speech long-hand and rehearsed it for hours. Even his "spontaneous" remarks were carefully crafted. F. E. Smith said, "Winston has spent the best years of his life writing impromptu speeches."

Churchill could be mockingly critical, but he was charitable when it mattered most. Upon the death of Neville Chamberlain, the prime minister whose policy of appeasement failed to prevent World War II, Churchill's eulogy rose above petty strivings: "Whatever else history may or may not say about these terrible, tremendous years, we can be sure that Neville Chamberlain acted with perfect sincerity according to his lights and strove to the utmost of his capacity and authority, which were powerful, to save the world from the awful devastating struggle in which we are now engaged."

Churchill's writings and speeches set excellent examples for any speech student, and his courage and truthfulness are an inspiring model for aspiring leaders of all ages. His perseverance in banishing fear, combined with his love of the English language, defeated Adolph Hitler. He is an extraordinary model for what any of us might do if we conquer our fears and stand courageously for what is right.

Attacking Fear Leads to Top Performance

In survey after survey, people rate speaking in front of a group as one of their worst fears. It ranks above fear of heights, insects and bugs, financial problems, deep water, sickness, flying, loneliness…and even death! In Chapter One, you learned about the remarkable blessings that good communication can bring into your life. In Chapter Two you will begin banishing fear so you can use your communication gifts to the fullest.

All my life I been afraid of high places. To help me conquer this fear, a climber friend volunteered to teach me how to rock climb. I was absolutely petrified the first time, but once I succeeded, my confidence soared. Attacking my fear of heights allowed me to pursue goals in a number of areas with new determination.

Secrets of Great Communicators uses proven strategies to subdue your fear of public speaking, turning dread into anticipation and nervousness into top performance. As you make you way through this chapter

• You will discover a six-step plan for working through your fears and turning them into a positive force.

- You will learn strategies for conquering all kinds of communication fear.

- You will acquire a new way to understand and work with people based on their communication styles.

- You will identify your personal communication style and become more well-rounded as a communicator.

Even if you don't personally face the fear of public speaking, you will benefit from this step by discovering why other people communicate as they do. You'll also learn to maximize your communication strengths in conversations and small group settings and how to tap into your individual source of passion so that great communication can flow. So, let's get to work defeating your fear and inspiring new confidence in your communication ability!

Fearful? You're Not the First!

The old shepherd squinted to protect his eyes from blowing dust as he gazed across the bleating flock of sheep. He often daydreamed about his former life. As the adopted son of the king's daughter, he had everything: a sparkling palace, servants catering to every whim, whatever he wanted. But now all was lost.

A fit of rage had gotten him into this mess. He happened upon a cruel master beating a slave, and he snapped. In his fury, he killed the man. Now he was a fugitive, running from the law by hiding in the desert.

"Just give me one chance," thought the shepherd, "and I'll do *anything* to make it right." Adjusting his gaze, his aching, watery eyes suddenly focused on a bizarre sight: a scrawny desert bush, burning.

He blinked. The bush was burning, all right, but it was not burning up. *The fire was being fueled by something other than the bush itself!* The shepherd shivered in fear, partly from the strange sight and partly from the chilling realization that he was probably losing his mind. Then the voice of God spoke, coming out of everywhere, yet nowhere: "Moses, take off your shoes. This is holy ground."

Wouldn't it be great to have God himself speak to you *out loud* about what He wants you to do with your life? You would think everyone would feel that way, but when Moses got his answer, he rejected it. Why? "Please Lord, I have never been eloquent—either in the past or recently or since You have been speaking to Your seravnt—because I am slow and hesitant in speech" (Exodus 4:10). In other words, "I cannot accomplish this mission because it involves communication skills I don't have."

Wait. Stop everything.

Did Moses really refuse the *God of the universe* because he lacked confidence in his speaking ability?

> "Never give in, never give in, never, never, never, never—in nothing, great or small, large or petty—never give in except to convictions of honor and good sense."
>
> —Winston Churchill

"...the morrow of such a victory as we have gained is a splendid moment both in our small lives and in our great history. It is a time not only of rejoicing but even more of resolve. When we look back on all the perils through which we have passed and at the mighty foes we have laid low and all the dark and deadly designs we have frustrated, why should we fear for our future?"

—Winston Churchill
After the German and Japanese surrender in World War II

Fortunately, God had mercy and replied, "Who made the human mouth? Who makes him mute or deaf, seeing or blind? Is it not I, the Lord? Now go! I will help you speak and I will teach you what to say" (Exodus 4:11-12)

A World of Purpose, Influence, Opportunity, and Excitement Awaits You

The fear that bound Moses binds all but a few today. Yet for those who are willing, a new world is waiting—a world of purpose, influence, opportunity, and excitement. Once you master your dread of public speaking, you will conquer fear after fear, embrace God's many purposes for your life, and unleash your gifts for significant impact.

As God admonished Joshua, "Be strong and courageous. Do not be afraid or discouraged, for the Lord your God is with you wherever you go" (Joshua 1:9). You have nothing to fear but fear itself!

What Sets Courageous People Apart?

Adam and Eve had it easy. No shame, no fear, no intimidation. They must have been like little children, excitedly chattering about all of the discover-ies they had made, making God laugh with appreciation when He visited them. In a fallen world, though, it is difficult to discover—let alone be confident of—God's purpose for your life. Fear and uncertainty lie just below the surface, intent on convincing you that you are not equipped to do great things for God.

Yonsa Boyahoo overcame her fear. As a child, she felt called to be a missionary, but her older brother, an army officer, strongly opposed the idea and admonished her, "Yonsa, do you not realize that you are ruining your life?" To which Yonsa replied, "My loving brother, you think you are so important as a lieutenant in the army of a king with two million subjects. I am a lieutenant in the army of the *king of kings.* How dare you tell me that what I do is insignificant?"

As a missionary, Yonsa quietly devoted her life to serving the poor in India. You've probably heard of Yonsa by the name she chose among the Sisters of Charity: Mother Teresa of Calcutta.

Courage is not the absence of fear but action in spite of fear. Courageous people develop an unshakable trust in God and wholeheartedly embrace the challenges God gives them.

How, though, does this work out in everyday life? In this chapter you'll discover that everyone—even those who are uncomfortable with public speaking—have hidden reservoirs of communication strength. Not only will you find out what your particular strengths are, but you'll also learn how to use them to compensate for your weaknesses. Believe it or not, some of the most successful public speakers are those who excelled at other types of communication and simply transferred their strengths to the public speaking arena. I'll show you how to do the same for yourself. Finally, you'll complete a "Conquering Public Speaking Anxiety" worksheet to help you logically analyze your fears and conquer them one by one.

Public Speaking Isn't the Only Communication Style

To truly succeed at something you must discover your strengths (and build on them) as well as your weaknesses (and compensate for them). Most of the time when people fail to capitalize on significant opportunities, it is because they are not aware of how to maximize their strengths and minimize their weaknesses.

The same is true with communication skills. A person may be skilled at public speaking but uncomfortable leading meetings. Or a person may be gifted at one-on-one communication but unable to move a crowd. According to communication scholar Dr. James C. McCroskey, there are four types of communication skills. The first, *speaking in groups,* deals with your communication in a group setting, such as a party. *Communication in meetings* ad-

dresses how you lead and interact with others in a formal meeting. *Conversation skill* is your communication one-on-one with another person. Finally, *public speaking* is how you speak in front of a group.

It is rare for someone to excel in all four types of communication although effective leaders gain some level of mastery over each one. People who are exceptioinally good public speakers may find it difficult to interact in small groups when they are not the center of attention. Conversely, those who relish one-on-one conversations may feel intimidated at being the focus as a speaker.

What does this mean to you? If you can tap into your God-given reservoir of communication strength, you will be able to

• Stop feeling guilty about your lack of confidence in some communication situations, freeing you up to spend more time on what you are good at.

• Build your strengths to compensate for your weaknesses. For example, Winston Churchill was extremely gifted with the written word. He used this ability to craft magnificent speeches and to cement his reputation as one of the 20th Century's greatest speakers.

• Recognize the strengths and weaknesses of others and help them improve in their communication ability. [A leadership tip: If you *really*

> "We make a living by what we get, but we make a life by what we give."
>
> —Winston Churchill

> "One mark of a great man is the power of making lasting impressions upon the people he meets."
>
> —Winston Churchill

want to be viewed as a leader, equip your followers to achieve success!]

Dr. McCroskey has developed a communication style quiz to help you understand in which communication situations you are most comfortable. It is called the *Personal Report of Communication Apprehension* (PRCA), and it is used here by his permission. You can take it yourself.

Discover the Source of Your Apprehension

The PRCA will help you determine the level of communication apprehension you feel in various situations. Please indicate in the box next to each question the degree to which you agree or disagree with each statement by writing the number associated with that response (*1= Strongly agree, 2= Agree, 3 = Undecided, 4 = Disagree, 5 = Strongly disagree*). At the end, you will calculate your score and gauge your strength in each type of communication.

1.   [ ] I dislike participating in group discussion.

2.   [ ] Usually I am calm and relaxed while participating in meetings.

3.   [ ] Ordinarily I am very tense and nervous in conversations.

4.   [ ] I have no fear of giving a speech.

5.   [ ] Generally, I am comfortable while participating in a group discussion.

6.   [ ] I am afraid to express myself at meetings.

7.   [ ] I feel relaxed while giving a speech.

8.   [ ] I have no fear of speaking up in conversation.

9.   [ ] Certain parts of my body feel very tense and rigid while giving a speech.

10.   [ ] While participating in a conversation with a new acquaintance, I feel very nervous.

11.   [ ] I like to get involved in group discussions.

12.   [ ] I am very relaxed when answering questions at a meeting.

13.   [ ] Ordinarily I am very calm and relaxed in conversations.

14.   [ ] Engaging in a group discussion with new people makes me tense and nervous.

15.   [ ] While giving a speech I get so nervous, I forget facts I really know.

16.   [ ] Generally, I am nervous when I have to participate in a meeting.

17. [ ] While conversing with a new acquaintance, I feel very relaxed.

18. [ ] I am tense and nervous while participating in group discussions.

19. [ ] I face the prospect of giving a speech with confidence.

20. [ ] Communicating at meetings usually makes me uncomfortable.

21. [ ] I'm afraid to speak up in conversations.

22. [ ] I am calm and relaxed while participating in group discussions.

23. [ ] I am very calm and relaxed when I am called on to express an opinion at a meeting.

24. [ ] My thoughts become confused and jumbled when I am giving a speech.

Here is how to calculate your score:

Talking in groups:

[ ] + [ ] + [ ] + 18
– [ ] – [ ] – [ ] = [ ]
(scores for items 5, 11, and 22)
(scores for items 1, 14, and 18)

Meetings:

[ ] + [ ] + [ ] + 18
– [ ] – [ ] – [ ] = [ ]
(scores for 2, 12, and 23)
(scores for 6, 16, and 20)

Conversation:

[ ] + [ ] + [ ] + 18
– [ ] – [ ] – [ ] = [ ]
(scores for 8, 13, and 17)
(scores for 3, 10, and 21)

Public speaking:

[ ] + [ ] + [ ] + 18
– [ ] – [ ] – [ ] = [ ]
(scores for 4, 7, and 19)
(scores for 9, 15, and 24)

TOTAL (of all four categories): [   ]

What This Quiz Means

The higher your score in each category, the more you seem to feel apprehensive about it. People with a total score higher than 83 are considered to be highly apprehensive in communication situations, whereas people who score lower than 55 are considered to be very unapprehensive in communication situations. People with scores between 55 and 83 are considered "moderate" in apprehension. It is completely normal to be more apprehensive in some areas and less apprehensive in others.

No matter what your score, you can build on your strengths and compensate for your weaknesses. Everyone lives with some level of communication fear, whether of public speaking, one-on-one conversations, groups, or meetings.

> "Things do not get better by being left alone. Unless they are adjusted, they explode with a shattering detonation"
>
> —Winston Churchill

In my years of communication coaching, I have discovered that the best way to help people become great public speakers is to *find their natural communication styles and duplicate them in front of an audience.* Let's take a look at how to do this in your life.

How to Use Your Communication Strengths to Compensate For Your Weaknesses

Through steadfast determination I conquered my own fear of public speaking. However, if I had to choose, my favorite communication situation is not public speaking, but one-on-one conversation. I dislike meetings and group discussions. You could say that I feel apprehensive in these situations. Since I cannot avoid them, here's what I do:

(1) Since my real strength is conversation, I focus on making my speaking style conversational. I have found that I gain strength as a public speaker by talking to an audience one person at a time.

(2) Since meetings are unavoidable, I try to take a leadership role so I can manage them efficiently and make them as short as possible.

(3) Since social gatherings are a valuable time to relax—or to make new

contacts and grow my business— I think in advance of questions to ask, and I try to engage folks in one-on-one conversation so we are not standing around in awkward silence.

These three steps allow me to master my fears and become more comfortable in communication situations where I feel out of place.

Build Rapport By Addressing Your Fears

After studying communication fear for a few years, I came to the realization that almost everyone experiences some level of fear. Many people fear communication in general while others fear not being in control of a situation. I have personified five common types of fear through fictional individuals: Sasha, Michael, Antonio, Chamille, and Benjamin. As you read about each, notice how a few simple steps could turn their fears into confidence. First, try to identify your own communication style in one of the five. Next, try to find the communication styles of those you live and work with. As you understand where they are coming from, it will be easier to gain their trust and influence them positively.

Communicator #1: The Entertainer

Sasha loves to speak in front of groups. She loves to see audience members laugh or cry as a result of her persuasive style and eloquence. One thing troubles her and confuses others when she's off the platform, however. Sasha has difficulty relating to people one-on-one. After a successful speech, she finds it difficult to concentrate on the needs of those who come up to ask questions or to seek advice. In addition, Sasha absolutely *hates* meetings. She considers it a waste of time to sit around while people "pool their ignorance." Obviously, Sasha's colleagues are put off by her seeming brashness and lack of concern.

Analysis: Sasha is gifted at public speaking, but focusing on her gifts and thoughts will make it hard for her to understand her audience. This could limit her effectiveness as a public speaker since she comes across as rude or condescending in interpersonal relationships.

Sasha could address this problem by focusing on the needs of others. Rather than simply asking, "What do *I* want to say?" she could ask, "What are the concerns and needs of this other person, or the audience, and how can I express my thoughts based on those concerns?" By turning her attention to others, Sasha would greatly enhance her impact.

Communicator #2: The Concerned Observer

Michael hates speaking in front of groups. It makes him so nervous he has trouble eating and sleeping the night before a presentation. When he speaks, he does not see the audience as a group, but as a collection of individuals, all of whom have separate needs, wants, and desires.

Michael finds himself planning for hours, sometimes focusing on one minor aspect of a speech, worrying that it will not communicate to each individual as he intends. He often comes across as tentative and uncertain when he speaks because he tries not to say anything that would offend anyone in the audience. This is true in meetings as well. He wants to make sure everyone has a chance to give input, so sometimes the meetings he runs take longer than scheduled and don't arrive at clearcut conclusions.

On the other hand, when the presentation or meeting is over and people come up to chat, Michael really feels at home. He loves to hear their concerns and to make people feel better about themselves.

Analysis: Michael is gifted at caring about the needs and concerns of others. Unfortunately, when he tries to take all of these concerns into account, Michael can't focus on what is most important.

To improve as a public speaker, Michael should focus on the *main point* he wants to communicate, and then choose two or three examples to help communicate that point to the audience. People are very different, but their experiences are similar enough that a speaker can communicate effectively through general examples and stories.

> "We shall go on to the end, we shall fight in France, we shall fight on the seas and oceans, we shall fight with growing confidence and growing strength in the air, we shall defend our island, whatever the cost may be, we shall fight on the beaches, we shall fight on the landing grounds, we shall fight in the fields and in the streets, we shall fight in the hills; we shall never surrender."
>
> —Winston Churchill
> **After becoming Prime Minister of Great Britain during World War II**

> "In my belief, you cannot deal with the most serious things in the world unless you also understand the most amusing."
>
> —Winston Churchill

In interpersonal communication, Michael could become more influential by focusing first on what he wishes to communicate and then by using his ability to relate to others to get the point across more effectively.

Communicator #3: The Life of the Party

Antonio loves meetings and conversations in small groups. He is often the star of parties because he naturally entertains groups of people with stories and jokes. People gather around Antonio wherever he goes, and he is skillful at including everyone in the interaction.

When people come to him one-on-one, however, he finds it difficult to concentrate on what they are saying. He looks for openings in the conversation where he can tell a story or relate an experience from his own life. This frustrates Antonio's co-workers because they find it difficult to get to the heart of a matter with him. In addition, Antonio's personable style does not work well in front of a larger audience. He comes across as being nervous because the mannerisms and techniques he uses to include others in conversation seem awkward when he is on the platform by himself.

Analysis: Antonio is gifted at group communication, but his challenge as a public speaker is that he views speaking as a different kind of communication, requiring a different style. To improve, Antonio should focus on "being himself" in front of an audience. He can do this by encouraging feedback, asking questions, and involving his audience in his speech.

In interpersonal situations, Antonio can improve by making it his goal to learn as much as he can from the other person. He could do this by asking for the other person's opinion on an issue, re-stating what the other person says, and disciplining himself to concentrate on the thoughts of others.

Communicator #4: The Contributor

Chamille cannot recall a time when she was ever nervous about communication. Whether in front of an audience, one-on-one, or in groups, she can always think of something to say. When in school, Chamille was always the first to raise her hand when the teacher asked a question. Sometimes she blurted out her response without raising her hand at all. If the teacher did not call on her, Chamille turned to someone around her and shared what was on her mind.

Now, Chamille finds it impossible in meetings to let an issue be discussed without her input. Sometimes, however, Chamille is baffled by others' response to her. When she talks a lot, they look at her as if they wish she would be quiet. She occasionally notices people rolling their eyes when she raises her hand or interrupts a conversation.

Analysis: Chamille's gift is the ability to relate quickly her experiences and concerns about the matter at hand.

She has a hard time, though, considering others' experiences and concerns as valid as her own. In public speaking, Chamille is gifted at getting her point across, but she could be more effective if she asked members of the audience to share their experiences and incorporated those into the point she wishes to communicate. By involving the audience, she could eventually become more comfortable with the idea that people can *learn* without her necessarily having to *teach* them.

In interpersonal communication, Chamille would benefit from being sensitive to the level of communication that the other person desires. *More communication is not necessarily better.* By choosing her points carefully in meetings and then remaining quiet while others contribute, Chamille would avoid frustrating others through her excessive contributions.

Communicator #5: The Reluctant Communicator

Benjamin really admires people who find communication to be natural and easy because he cannot imagine *any* communication situation in which he would be comfortable. It terrifies him to speak in front of groups, no matter how big or small. Once in anticipation of a presentation, Benjamin felt sick to his stomach for three days beforehand.

In meetings, Benjamin's boss has to prompt him repeatedly to give input because Benjamin would prefer to be silent and listen to what others have to say. Even a knock on the door or the ring of the telephone causes his heart to jump since he does not know who might be there and what they might want. In fact, Benjamin nearly failed to graduate from college because he did not want to take the required speech course. The only reason he got his current job is because the interviewer saw past Benjamin's shattered nerves and recognized his technical skill.

Analysis: Many people like Benjamin are able to conquer their fear of public speaking by (1) writing down their fears and analyzing them objectively, (2) speaking *only* on subjects they care about, (3) getting advice and feedback on their speech material in advance of giving the speech, and (4) preparing for the speech by practicing the speech aloud, both by themselves and in front of a trusted friend.

In meetings, Benjamin should try to discern the purpose of the discussion in advance and jot some notes about points he thinks should be covered. In the meeting itself, he should ask questions, suggest particular issues for discussion, and make a few brief remarks, all without drawing too much attention to himself (undue attention is what makes him most nervous).

In interpersonal communication, Benjamin should take steps to prepare in advance as well. He could think of three or four generic questions to ask during a lull in conversation. In his job, he could improve by asking for feedback from his co-workers and boss. This feedback will assure him that he is

"I was very glad that Mr. Attlee described my speeches in the war as expressing the will not only of Parliament but of the whole nation. Their will was resolute and remorseless and, as it proved, unconquerable. It fell to me to express it, and if I found the right words you must remember that I have always earned my living by my pen and by my tongue. It was a nation and a race dwelling all round the globe that had the lion heart. I had the luck to be called upon to give the roar."

—Winston Churchill
At his 80th birthday celebration

> "The destiny of mankind is not decided by material computation. When great causes are on the move in the world...we learn that we are spirits, not animals, and that something is going on in space and time, and beyond space and time, which, whether we like it or not, spells duty."
>
> —Winston Churchill

on the right course and will reduce his fear of talking with these people.

As you can see, individuals are very different in their life experiences, gifts, and interests. Employ the strategies offered in the video coaching lesson and in these case studies, and you'll manage your fear without losing your distinctiveness.

The Best Fear-Conquering Strategy of All

If you still feel apprehensive about giving a speech, you'll be happy to know that I've saved the very best fear-conquering tool for last.

Here it is: ***Take pride in your fear.***

That's right! From God's perspective being weak is actually a *good* thing. The Apostle Paul recognized his weaknesses and asked God to take them away. God's answer was "My grace is sufficient for you, for power is perfected in weakness" (2 Corinthians 12:9). In light of God's direction, Paul wrote, "Therefore I will most gladly boast all the more about my weaknesses, so that Christ's power may reside in me.... For when I am weak, then I am strong" (2 Corinthians 12:9-10). As long as you are willing to obey God, you can rest assured that He will turn your weakness into strength.

You have been made in God's image. He has imparted tremendous gifts to you. But as a result of sin, weaknesses and faults disrupt your work and your relationships with other people. God, in his mercy, uses these weaknesses, as well as your strengths—to mold you into what He wants you to be.

So, don't be discouraged if you are not as gifted at certain types of communication as other people you know. Rather, pray that God will give you the strength to use *your* gifts to the best of your ability and the humility to see how He is glorified through your weaknesses.

Three Steps to Take Right Now

You will find detailed below three valuable steps to boost your confidence and set you on the road to powerful public speaking.

1. Personal Application.

In this chapter, you analyzed your strong points and weak areas in various types of communication. You also learned about five communication patterns and how each has strengths which help compensate for its weaknesses. Now this personal application is your opportunity to bring these together and apply the lessons to yourself.

By understanding your communication assets and liabilites, you will see where to start your journey of self-improvement. You can nurture your strengths even as you compensate for your weaknesses.

2. "Conquering Public Speaking Anxiety" Worksheet.

In the video coaching lesson, I introduced six steps to overcoming the fear of public speaking. This worksheet will give you the opportunity to think about and to write down your fears so you can address them one by one.

And believe me, this worksheet really works! I have used it countless times as a public speaking coach to help students deal rationally with their fears. I even have used it myself when giving new speeches or facing novel situations. Remember, the monsters in your head are much less powerful when you get them on paper. Write down your fears and watch them shrink!

3. Heroes Speech Project.

You will have the opportunity to write and deliver a short presentation on an admirable hero from history. We looked earlier at the heroic life of Mother Teresa, a woman who gained admiration and respect because of her determination to submit to God's will and to let Him shape her influence on the world. As I studied her life, I grew in boldness. Thinking about the heroic qualities of others will inspire you and give you strength to persevere through difficulties.

The "Heroes Speech Project" is "win-win" for you and your audience. Your hero's courage will encourage you to overcome fear *and* it will impress your audience. I've seen it happen time and time again.

Use the speech outline and sample speech as a guide, and I assure you that your audience will want to hear your speech from start to finish, even if you are nervous. Doing this will lift your spirits and prepare you for Chapter Three of *Secrets of Great Communicators*.

Best wishes to you as you banish your fear and find a new level of communication confidence!

"Don't be too careless about yourselves—on the other hand not too careful. Live well but do not flaunt it. Laugh a little and teach your men to laugh—get good humor under fire—war is a game that's played with a smile. If you can't smile, grin. If you can't grin, keep out of the way till you can."

—Winston Churchill
Advice to his commanders during World War II

Personal Application

1. **Here are four lists of reasons people enjoy various communication situations. Look through each list, and check (√) every item you personally enjoy. Put an "x" next to the ones in which you feel you could improve. You also may want to add reasons of your own to the lists.**

Talking in Groups

[X] Debating an interesting topic.

[√] Participating in a fast-moving discussion.

[√] Comparing my experiences with others.

[√] Hanging out with people I like.

[√] Making plans with a few other people.

[√] Observing how people interact with each other.

[√] Making what I have to say interesting so people keep listening.

[X] Telling stories to make other people laugh.

[X] Asking questions of a person that others are curious about.

[ ] Other:_____

Meetings

[√] Giving my opinion about something.

[√] Challenging other people to do something.

[√] Reporting information to others.

[ ] Talking about something in-depth.

[ ] Having an orderly flow to the discussion.

[ ] Participating in group decision-making.

[X] Listening to what others think.

[ ] Being around interesting people.

[ ] Arriving at meaningful decisions as a group.

[ ] Other:_____

Interpersonal (one-on-one)

[x] Learning why people think as they do.

[ ] Meeting a new person.

[ ] Having an opportunity to talk about my ideas.

[ ] Catching up on the latest news.

[ ] Sharing personal information.

[x] Being able to find out new things about the other person.

[ ] Showing concern for the other person.

[ ] Being able to relax and enjoy a conversation.

[x] Listening carefully to what the other person says.

[ ] Other:_____

Public Speaking

[ ] Having my thoughts and interests be the center of attention.

[x] Being able to persuade people of what I think.

[ ] Getting people to respond emotionally to what I say.

[ ] Motivating people to feel confident in themselves.

[x] Saying something clever to make people think.

[x] Making people laugh.

[ ] Teaching new information.

[ ] Giving information without interruption.

[ ] Having people appreciate what I know.

"Come on now all you young men, all over the world. You have not an hour to lose. You must take your places in Life's fighting line.... Raise the glorious flags again, advance them upon the new enemies, who constantly gather upon the front of the human army, and have only to be assaulted to be overthrown....You will make all kinds of mistakes; but as long as you are generous and true, and also fierce, you cannot hurt the world or even seriously distress her."

—Winston Churchill
Advice to his commanders during World War II

2. Of the statements you checked (√), on the next page, write in the space below the four you enjoy most. Brainstorm how this strength can compensate for one of the communication weaknesses next to which you placed an "x". For example:

I enjoy...	How to use what I enjoy to compensate for what I do not enjoy:
Group Communication: I enjoy participating in a fast-moving discussion	Public Speaking: I could use this strength to ask the audience stimulating questions and guide the discussion toward a conclusion
Public Speaking: I enjoy getting other people to respond emotionally to what I say.	Meetings: I could use this strength by thinking of one brief, stimulating story or example to use to make my point in a meeting.
Interpersonal Communication: I enjoy listening carefully to what the other person says.	Group Communication: I could use this strength by asking others for their views of my topic and listening to what they say before I speak.
Meetings: I enjoy arriving at meaningful decisions as a group.	Interpersonal Communication: I could use this strength by asking the other person for feedback about decisions I must make.

Now try it for yourself:

I enjoy...	How to use what I enjoy to compensate for what I do not enjoy:

"If you have an important point to make, don't try to be subtle or clever. Use a pile driver. Hit the point once. Then come back and hit it again. Then hit it a third time—a tremendous whack."

—Winston Churchill

I enjoy...	How to use what I enjoy to compensate for what I do not enjoy:

Conquering Public Speaking Anxiety Worksheet

(Make photocopies of this form and use it each time you give a speech to help you overcome your fears)

1. Identify the source of your anxiety.

What specifically makes you uncomfortable about this situation? For example, "I fear that the audience won't like my speech." List as many sources as you can think of.

2. Take each of the fears listed above and explain it in a positive way.

For example, "I will begin the speech with a suspenseful story and wait until the end of the speech to tell the audience what happened. This will help me keep their attention."

3. Focus on the audience, not yourself.

List all of the concerns, expectations, and characteristics of the audience you can think of and decide on a strategy to address each. For example "The audience will be very tired, having just finished a long week, so I want to make my remarks brief, to the point, and cheery."

4. Invest time in preparation.

List the areas where you feel you could benefit from preparation. Remember, preparation does not mean just writing out your notes. It also means practicing the speech aloud.

5. Speak only on subjects you care about.

List several subjects about which you are passionate and that are relevant to the audience. Ask several people which topics they find most interesting and what they would like to know about each.

6. Develop a sense of mission.

Write out a mission statement that conveys the importance of what you wish to communicate to the audiecne. For example, "I will be speaking about how to stay healthy in the workplace. This audience desperately wants and needs to hear this information because getting sick at work makes them feel miserable and unproductive."

Heroes Speech Project

Throughout Chapter Two, Winston Churchill has been our inspiration for overcoming obstacles and courageously influencing the world. In this biographical speech project, you become familiar with, and express to others, the wonderful heritage that a heroic figure provides. The project will help you tune your senses to the heroes whose character qualities are worth emulating. In the process, you will begin to form your own model of leadership and recognize that people become heroic through their conformity to the character of Christ.

The goal of this project is to research and prepare a five minute speech on a leader who meets the "What is a hero?" criteria in the sidebar on the previous page. When your speech is complete, find several places to give it for practice—a class, your church, or even a community group. This is your opportunity to bless others while sharpening your own skills. Here are some guidelines:

1. Choose a person who is not mentioned in the Bible.

The goal of this speech project is to expose you to the ordinary people who lived *after* Bible times and who accomplished great things for Christ.

2. Avoid giving a speech about someone you know personally.

Broaden your horizons by focusing on figures from the past who can be studied through historical writings.

3. Do your research!

Choose a figure who is featured in books, magazines, essays, or encyclopedias. *Draw from at least three sources.*

4. Use at least one actual quote in your speech.

If possible, choose a quote from the person's speeches, writings, or journal entries.

In the following pages you will find an outline for your speech, a sample biographical speech, and several tips about heroic qualities and famous heroes from Christian history. Once you have looked over these materials, create the outline for your speech on a separate sheet of paper.

Where to find out about heroes:

• **INTERNET**

Search by such keywords as "biographies" or "Christian biographies."

• **BOOKS**

Dictionary of Christianity in America (InterVarsity Press), *Foxe's Book of Martyrs* (Fleming Revell Publishers).

• **BIOGRAPHY SERIES**

Both Youth with a Mission and Bethany House publish dozens of biographies of great Christians.

• **MAGAZINES**

Each issue of *Christian History* magazine features in-depth biographies of notable believers.

Heroes Speech Outline

Character qualities worth focusing on:

Alertness
Boldness
Compassion
Contentment
Creativity
Dependability
Determination
Diligence
Discernment
Endurance
Enthusiasm
Faith
Flexibility
Forgiveness
Generosity
Hospitality
Humility
Joyfulness
Justice
Love
Loyalty
Meekness
Obedience
Patience
Persuasiveness
Security
Self-control
Sincerity
Tolerance
Truthfulness
Virtue
Wisdom

1. INTRODUCTION

A. Attention Device. Carefully plan your first 50 words to gain the audience's attention. Effective attention devices include examples, stories, personal experiences, shocking statements, or dramatic interpretations.

B. Relate the purpose of the speech. Relate the subject of the speech to yourself and the audience by establishing a strong topic sentence:

"The purpose of this speech is to _____ by

_____."

2. BODY

A. State the topic sentence. State the topic sentence at the beginning so the audience can organize your material in their minds. Be creative in the way you do this. Rather than just saying, "The purpose of this speech is...", you can say, "By examining the life of _____ I hope to show you _____."

B. Translate the topic sentence. Elaborate on the topic sentence by clearly explaining what you mean and what you believe are the central issues.

C. Exemplify the topic sentence. Expand on the topic sentence by using examples and stories from the person's life.

- Briefly describe his or her background

- Briefly describe his or her mission

- Share one or two key stories from the person's life which exemplify your topic sentence.

D. Prove the topic sentence. Use research to substantiate your conclusion. Vivid quotes from the person and quotes about the person usually serve this purpose quite well.

3. CONCLUSION

Provide a focus to your presentation and help the audience draw conclusions from your speech. Be certain to relate the conclusion to your introduction and to your topic sentence.

A few heroes from Christian history:

Thomas Aquinas
Augustine
Gladys Aylward
J. S. Bach
William Blackstone
Dietrich Bonhoeffer
John Bunyan
John Calvin
Amy Carmichael
George Washington Carver
G. K. Chesterton
Calvin Coolidge
Fanny Crosby
Jonathan Edwards
George Frederick Handel
Joan of Arc
Francis Scott Key
C. S. Lewis
Abraham Lincoln
Martin Luther
D. L. Moody
Mother Teresa of Calcutta
George Müller
John Newton
Florence Nightingale
Blaise Pascal
Charles Spurgeon
Billy Sunday
Hudson Taylor
Corrie Ten Boom
Noah Webster
John Wesley
George Whitefield
William Wilberforce

Sample Speech

The following speech was given by a twelve-year-old young man as part of an oratorical contest. It contains many elements which appeal to an audience and which display good communication and organization skill.

Destiny: Choice, Not Chance

Someday, you are going to have something happen to you that you cannot control. A car accident. A physical problem. A fire. But whatever happens you will not be able to control it. You choose how this happening will affect your destiny and whether you have the courage and the drive to turn it into good.

For example, a young slave girl named Araminta Ross made a choice when she ran away from her master. She chose the nights alone in the swamps, the hunger, and the severe penalty if she were to be caught. She wanted to be free. She had to decide how to run away and then find the courage to do it.

Araminta was born a slave in the 1820's in Bucktown, Maryland. In 1844, while she was still a slave, she married John Tubman, who was a free black, and became the Harriet Tubman of our history books.

In the mid 1800's Harriet made her escape from slavery, via the underground railroad, to Philadelphia. When she became free, she vowed to go back to Maryland to help other slaves escape. Her first trip back to Maryland was a little while after Congress passed the fugitive slave act which made it against the law to assist runaway slaves. In the 1850's, Harriet led over 300 slaves to freedom. To do this, she had to outwit many slave hunters and their bloodhounds. Then, in 1857, Harriet led her parents to freedom.

Harriet made many choices and had many things happen that she could not control. But she worked hard and kept her eyes on her goal—freedom.

Half a century after Harriet Tubman died, fire scorched the destiny of an 8-year old Kansas school boy. The boy's legs were burned very badly in a schoolhouse fire. The doctors said that there was only one thing to do: amputate. The boy protested and his parents considered their choices. Finally, they decided to let the boy have his way—that even if he never walked again, he would still be a whole man. As the young boy lay in bed, he determined to walk again. The difficulty of fulfilling this desire was described by William Herman, who wrote *Run, Boy, Run!* Mr. Herman says, "The boy's legs were twisted sticks, his knees and shins were bare of flesh, the toes of his left foot were completely gone, and his transverse arch was practically destroyed."

In the spring when the bandages were removed, the boy's mother and father took turns rubbing his legs. When they were not available, he rubbed them himself. One day he announced, "In one week I am going to walk." When the day came, his doubtful father gently lowered him to the floor. The boy cried out, "I can feel the floor!" But when his father let go of him, he collapsed and was lifted back to his bed, sobbing. That was the first attempt. Daily the routine continued until the day when his father let him go and the boy felt a sharp pain as blood spurted into his deadened legs. He stood only for a few seconds, but it was the best few seconds of his life! Later, at the age of 13, this boy won his first foot race at a county fair, and later he went on to shatter many track records. Then, in 1949, Glenn Cunningham, the one who would never walk again, was acknowledged as the fastest man in the world!

Glenn's choice to keep his legs, his courage, and his hard work had paid off.

When chance alters your life in that car accident, fire, or physical problem, you must choose your destiny and have the courage and the fortitude to fulfill it.

Destiny: it is choice, not chance. It is up to you!

ORGANIZE YOUR TALK FOR MAXIMUM IMPACT

(31 minutes)

Three questions an audience asks about you:

1. Does this person know what he or she is _____ about?

2. Can we _____ this person?

3. Does this person really _____ about the subject and demonstrate why _____ should care?

How to show that you know what you are talking about:

S = _____
T = _____
    Definition: Clarify the _____ of the terms
    Explanation: Explain the _____
E = _____
    Example: Show the _____ and character of the rest
    Personal experience: Describe your own _____
    Analogy: _____ the unknown to the known
P = _____
    Testimony: An expert's _____
    Statistic: Numerical _____ of data

How to show that you can be trusted:
*   Slowly but _____

*   Reference your _____

*   Reference _____ authorities

*   Be well _____

*   Be _____

*   Temper your _____

How to convince the audience that you care—and that they should care too:
*   Attention-getting _____
    *
    *
*   Make the audience aware of their _____
*   Offer a viable _____
*   Visualize the solution _____
*   _____ the solution.

Organize Your Talk for Maximum Impact

Focus on Great Communicators:
Abraham Lincoln

CHAPTER AT A GLANCE

- Expertise is not enough.
- Time to lead? Better get organized!
- A taste of your own medicine.
- Just because you're right doesn't mean you're persuasive.
- Show me the money!
- Persuading your audience, **S.T.E.P.** by **S.T.E.P.**
- Dancing gracefully with evidence.
- How the **S.T.E.P.** system will transform your public presence.
- Moving your audience to action.
- Putting the persuasion formula together.
- Three steps to take right now.
- Your new, persuasive self.

ABRAHAM LINCOLN'S BEST-KNOWN speech is his 1863 dedication of the cemetery at Gettysburg. The address that began with "Four score and seven years ago" concluded: "We here highly resolve that these dead shall not have died in vain—that this nation, under God, shall have a new birth of freedom—and that government of the people, by the people, for the people, shall not perish from the earth."

Lincoln was unknown outside of Illinois until a few memorable speeches propelled him to the presidency. First, he spoke against compromise with pro-slavery forces in an address to the Illinois

> "I have only to say, let us discard all this quibbling about this man and the other man—this race and that race being inferior, and therefore they must be placed in an inferior position—discarding our standard that we have left us. Let us discard all these things, and unite as one people throughout this land, until we shall once more stand up declaring that all men are created equal."
>
> —**Abraham Lincoln,**
> Chicago, Illinois
> July 1858

Republican State Convention in 1858: "A house divided against itself cannot stand...I do not expect the Union to be dissolved...but I *do* expect it will cease to be divided."

Lincoln gave other decisive speeches during his 1858 race for the U. S. Senate against Stephen A. Douglas. Douglas characterized Lincoln as a dangerous extremist whose anti-slavery views were against the will of the Founding Fathers. In the face of Douglas' charges, Lincoln faltered at one point, but in the debate at Freeport he recovered and shrewdly issued challenges of his own. Although Douglas won the election that year, his response to Lincoln's arguments alienated the Southern states and, ironically, doomed his 1860 presidential bid against the very man he had defeated, Abraham Lincoln.

Another of Lincoln's momentous speeches took place before a New York abolition society. Lincoln's carefully reasoned arguments and self-effacing humor helped him gain support for the Republican nomination for the presidency. Lincoln told them, "Let us have faith that right makes might, and in that faith let us, to the end, dare to do our duty as we understand it." Deep division among the Democrats ensured Lincoln's victory, and seven southern states seceded from the Union. Throughout his presidency, Lincoln used his rhetorical ability to cast the war between the states as being about slavery rather than states rights, as the Southern states claimed.

Lincoln was assassinated only days after the Civil War ended, but the Republican party thrived. His influence as a great communicator strengthened the presidency, with both positive and negative results. One thing is clear, however. Because of his perseverance and timely speeches, Abraham Lincoln is honored as one of America's greatest presidents. His life shows that when you organize your thoughts clearly and take your main points (not yourself) seriously, you will be more successful in calling your audience to action.

Expertise is Not Enough

I suffered once under a college professor who had a nearly impossible time communicating. He began each class with some manner of obscure statement and proceeded downhill from there. The more he spoke, the more confused we became. Frustrated, this professor repeatedly disintegrated into incomplete sentences, obtuse arguments, and rapid-fire changes of subject. Daily, students left class bewildered.

By contrast, another of my professors clearly stated his purpose at the beginning of each class, outlined his goals, presented his lecture in an organized fashion, solicited feedback from students, and answered questions until he was certain we understood the concepts being presented.

Oddly, the faculty of our school revered the first professor, considering him brilliant. The second professor, on the other hand, was a lower-level, un-tenured lecturer. Yet we students didn't care. We avoided the first in every way possible because his lectures made us feel unintelligent. We embraced the second professor for precisely the opposite reason: he gave us confidence that we could understand and master the subject.

Fears of public speaking and rejection notwithstanding, audiences actually ask surprisingly little of a speaker. They want to know what the goal of the speech is. They want to see the speaker making progress toward that goal. They want to know how they personally will benefit by listening, and they want the speaker to care about them and empower them to act on what they hear. Few people, however, have patience with speeches that are difficult to follow. Faced with a disorganized speaker, most audiences simply "change channels" and tune out.

In this chapter, you will be introduced to the awesome power of logical organization. You'll discover how a well-ordered presentation helps you reach the heart of the audience. And best of all, you'll learn how to organize, whether or not you think of yourself as a "gifted" speaker. Here are the topics we will cover:

• Audiences ask three questions about you as a speaker, and the way you present yourself communicates whether or not they should listen.

Discover how to get a "yes" answer every time.

• Learn how to select the right kind of evidence to prove every point and how to give added power to examples, illustrations, statistics, and expert opinions.

• Build credibility by organizing your speech in a logical, easy-to-follow fashion. (This method can also transform your papers, reports, and essays and equip you to "think on your feet"!)

• It isn't your information that is persuasive as much as it is how organized it is. Find out what research shows to be the most effective way to inspire an audience to action.

Confidence and credibility await as you prepare to organize for maximum impact!

Time to Lead? Better Get Organized!

Nehemiah was cupbearer to King Artaxerxes, the most powerful monarch of his day. Nehemiah's job was to protect the king from death by poisoning. His position must have been very prestigious, since he was one of the few men who lived close to the king, visited him daily, and enjoyed the monarch's full confidence. Nehemiah had come far for someone whose compatriots first arrived in Babylon as prisoners.

> "I beg of you, as citizens of this great Republic, not to let your minds be carried off from the great work we have before us. This struggle is too large for you to be diverted from it by any small matter. When you return to your homes rise up to the height of a generation of men worthy of a free Government, and we will carry out the great work we have commenced."
>
> —Abraham Lincoln
> to the 164th Ohio regiment

> "We meet this evening, not in sorrow, but in gladness of heart...[with] hope of a righteous and speedy peace whose joyous expression cannot be restrained. In the midst of this, however, He, from Whom all blessings flow, must not be forgotten. A call for a national thanksgiving is being prepared, and will be duly promulgated."
>
> —Abraham Lincoln, speech upon the surrender of the Army of Virginia, four days before his death

When representatives arrived from Jerusalem, the city of his forefathers, Nehemiah asked how things were going there. The visitors told him the people were in great distress because the wall of the city had been destroyed, and as a result the citizens lived in fear and disgrace. It would have been easy for Nehemiah to say, "Gee, that's too bad, but I'm certainly not going to risk everything I've worked for to help you."

Instead, Nehemiah took the Jews' problems as his own. "When I heard these words," he wrote, "I sat down and wept. I mourned for a number of days, fasting and praying before the God of heaven" (Nehemiah 1:4).

After praying for repentance for himself and his people, Nehemiah acted, and his leadership demonstrates the power of preparation and the importance of organization. Nehemiah prepared a persuasive appeal to the king (2:4-5), assembled a list of resources necessary to rebuild the wall of Jerusalem (2:6-9), and personally inspected the condition of the wall before persuading the embattled citizens of Jerusalem to join him in rebuilding it (2:11-18).

Once construction got underway, his organizational and leadership skills grew further:

• He prioritized his tasks (3:1-5);

• He organized workers and delegated responsibilities (3:1-32);

• He encouraged the workers (4:13-14);

• He set a personal example of commitment (4:23, 5:15-18);

• He mediated conflicts between workers (5:1-14);

• He stayed focused (6:3);

• He dealt firmly with those opposed to the rebuilding (6:1-12).

With God's help, Nehemiah and his team completed the project—which had been on hold for 200 years—in 52 days. And he stepped into the history books as one of the most effective leaders of all time.

Nehemiah's inspirational leadership provides a compelling lesson for those who desire to be more influential communicators. He was passionate about his cause, persuasive, and quick-thinking. But most of all he was methodical and organized. He planned carefully, and as a result, people took him seriously.

Once you master the steps in this chapter, you, like Nehemiah, can employ organizational strategies, build credibility, and successfully reach the heart of your audience.

A Taste of Your Own Medicine

Imagine that, playing around with some chemicals one evening, you create a potion that transforms you into a genius. Within minutes you are speed reading, solving complex mathematical problems, and generally thinking brilliant thoughts. Days and weeks pass, and the effect remains without any complications. You send the potion to a respected laboratory for testing, and their results confirm that the mixture really does work. So, you give your formula a name: Mind Booster.

At this point, you would face a great challenge. How could Mind Booster be presented to the public? Most people would be highly skeptical, especially when you explain how you discovered the formula—by swallowing concoctions from your chemistry set.

What should you do? You could explain scientifically how Mind Booster achieves its miraculous results and offer a personal testimony of how it turned you into a genius. But most people would still not believe you.

You could show a credible, scientific study which demonstrates that the average person's I.Q. increases by 25 points after taking Mind Booster. You could even get medical doctors to testify to this fact. Lots of folks would be interested, but most would still refuse to take it. Do you know why?

Just Because You're Right Doesn't Mean You're Persuasive

Most people are not convinced simply because you are correct in your views.

You must show them their need, overcome their objections, and give them a reasonable way to act on your information. Persuasion is not so much *what* you say but *how* you say it. In this chapter, you'll take persuasion to the next level by learning how to use evidence, how to make it persuasive, and how to organize your speech for maximum impact. Along the way, you may discover how to market Mind Booster (or whatever you choose) and make a fortune!

Show Me the Money!

The word "evidence" comes from the Latin word *videre*, which means "to see." While *you* may see the truth of your message clearly enough, your audience wants proof. "Show me the money," they say, or, "Prove it." This is where evidence comes into play. Proper use of evidence transforms persuasive appeals in three ways:

1. Evidence makes you more credible.

The operative word here is "credibility" which comes from the word *creed*, meaning "to trust or believe." To be credible means the audience gives you the benefit of the doubt and is willing to hear what you have to say. Using evidence the right way gives both you and your message an edge.

> "Take all that you can of this book upon reason, and the balance on faith, and you will live and die a happier man."
>
> —Abraham Lincoln
> (about the Bible)

> "To correct the evils, great and small, which spring from want of sympathy and from positive enmity among strangers, as nations or as individuals, is one of the highest functions of civilization."
>
> —Abraham Lincoln

2. Evidence gets people to pay attention.

Remember the "Shannon-Weaver" model of communication from the first video coaching lesson? When a sender sends a message to the receiver, physical noise and psychological noise prevent the message from coming across as intended. This is solved by "redundancy"—making your case with several independent lines of evidence. You may offer personal experiences, quotes from a noted authority, examples, and compelling statistics. Using multiple forms of support helps convince skeptics while reinforcing the commitment of those already persuaded.

3. Evidence helps you deliver your message to the heart.

To persuade an audience, you must relate your message to what the audience already understands and believes. In the mid-20th century, a researcher named George Miller wrote about the "70/30 Principle." He noted that only 30% of your message should contain new information. The rest should tie the new information into what the audience already knows. Definitions, explanations, examples, personal experience, analogies, testimonies, and statistics are foot soldiers who charge through the noise to capture the attention of the audience.

Evidence is the raw material for persuasion, but it must be refined through proper organization to become convincing.

Persuading Your Audience S. T. E. P. by S. T. E. P.

The S. T. E. P. system is an easy-to-remember way of organizing evidence. I first learned about S. T. E. P. from Dr. Lee Polk, professor of speech at Baylor University. In the video lesson, I showed how the S. T. E. P. system makes your speech more clear and believable. It leads your audience from understanding your point, to perceiving its relevance, to believing it to be true. Let's review each part of the S. T. E. P. system and how it can work for you.

S = State

Effective speakers begin each point by stating it clearly. Have you ever listened to a confusing speaker, who, at the very end of the speech, said, "I guess what I'm trying to say is _____." You may have wondered, "Why didn't he say so in the first place?" Stating your point clearly is how you "say so in the first place."

T = Translate

Translating your point means you transfer your understanding of the topic to the audience, usually done through giving definitions of key terms, explaining your point more fully, or both.

Defining Key Terms

"Defining" means to clarify the meaning of specific terms. An obvious first step, it is often overlooked. You should never assume the audience understands an important word the same way you do. By defining the key terms, you bring the audience to view the subject from your perspective.

A great deal of your case rests on how you define key terms. Once, while debating family policy, my opponent claimed that the "traditional family" is obsolete. Disagreeing, I asked, "What do you mean by *traditional family*?" My opponent replied, "A family with a father who works, a mother who stays home, and two children." Since that definition seemed to me much too narrow, I defined *traditional family* as "any family which adheres to traditional values," a much broader definition which encompasses a greater percentage of the population. If I had not taken pains to question my opponent's definition and offer one of my own, I could not have refuted his point.

In a class I was teaching, I once got into a discussion of whether it was appropriate for Christians to harbor Jews in World War II Europe and to lie when confronted by Nazis. Some students argued that it was wrong to lie under any circumstance. Other students replied that lying to save lives is appropriate. I interrupted the discussion to point out that the argument is not really about whether it is appropriate to lie, but about what *constitutes* a lie: If a lie means "telling an untruth to someone who is *owed* the truth," then the ethics of the situation can be seen in a different light. The Nazis were not owed the truth. Because they stood for an evil cause, their opponents were obligated to mislead and deceive them whenever possible. Such is the nature of war. Again, by defining "lie," we were able to discuss the issue more fruitfully.

Socrates said, "If you wish to debate with me, you must first define your terms." Defining the terms is paramount to winning debates. *Always provide clear definitions of your terms at the outset.*

Explaining Your Point More Fully

To "explain" something literally means to "bring it out on the plain" where it is clear and intelligible. Speakers explain their point by devoting two or three sentences to elaborating on what they mean, usually starting with one of the following phrases:

- "In other words…"

- "What I mean by that is…"

For example: "At issue in the debate over the proper role of government is whether America is a democracy or a republic. In other words, we must understand whether the Founding Fathers intended for the people to rule and

> "I should be glad if I could flatter myself that I came as near to the central idea of the occasion in two hours as you did in two minutes."
>
> —Edward Everett, the speaker who preceded Abraham Lincoln on the platform just prior to the Gettysburg Address, speaking to Lincoln

> "Considering the great degree of modesty which should always attend youth, it is probable I have already been more presuming than becomes me. However...holding it a sound maxim, that it is better to be only sometimes right, than at all times wrong, so soon as I discover my opinions to be erroneous, I shall be ready to renounce them."
>
> —Abraham Lincoln, candidate for the Illinois state legislature at age 23

make the decisions directly or whether they intended a representative form of government in which people would elect leaders to make decisions on their behalf."

E = Exemplify

To exemplify something is to illustrate it or show it by example. Exemplifying a point makes the point more personal, bringing it alive for the audience. Three ways to exemplify your point are: *example*, *personal experience*, and *analogy*.

Example

An example is a "real world" confirmation of your conclusion. An example can convey the intensity of a problem and can make clear the effectiveness of your proposed solution. Examples start with words like:

- "For example…"

- "Take, for instance…"

- "Let's examine the case of…"

To exemplify: "As political figures become more corrupt, people long for a leader who is strong, yet gracious, firm, yet merciful. Perhaps we would be inspired by the real-life example of King Alfred, ruler of Britain in the late 800s A.D. He not only won freedom from Danish oppression, but he was instrumental in the conversion of the Danish king, Guthram, to Christianity."

Personal Experience

A personal experience is an example from one's own life. When you share an experience clearly, people in your audience feel almost as if the experience is their own. Audiences relish personal experiences; it is not uncommon for a person to remember a speaker's story for years and recall the point associated with it. The *Chicken Soup for the Soul* book series became a publishing phenomenon by recording and retelling stories which inspired people to be more compassionate toward others.

Analogy

An analogy compares the *unknown* to the *known*. Analogies are the primary way we describe unfamiliar ideas or objects to others. Think about how you would describe peanut butter to someone from a culture which had neither peanuts nor butter. You would probably compare peanuts to a nut with which the people are familiar, describing how to crush the nuts and mix them with oil to create a paste. This is exemplifying a concept through an analogy.

It is difficult, if not impossible, to learn something new without using analogies. Missionaries translating the gospel in a remote jungle, for example, discovered that the tribe with which they were working had no animal resembling a sheep. Therefore, to say, "All we like sheep have gone astray" meant nothing to them. To bridge the communication gap, the missionaries observed animals familiar to the natives, assessed their characteristics, and chose one to serve as a substitute in their translation of Scripture. *That* is an analogy.

Analogies surround us. When you describe a new author to a friend, you usually begin with, "Her books are sort of like…." Describing a new food, you might say, "Have you ever had a ____? It is kind of like that." These are analogies, and many times we cannot communicate without them.

Analogies are vitally important to establishing your point in a speech. In fact, to *think* in analogies demostrates an astounding comprehension of the complex relationships among things. The prolific inventor Thomas Edison attributed his success to an ability to think in analogies. He took abstract ideas and compared them to things he already understood. Therefore, he perceived far more than others and put those perceptions to work. During his career, Edison, on average, achieved a minor invention every ten days and a major one, such as the phonograph and electric light bulb, every six months!

P = Prove

Audiences may be pleased when you describe your main point in easy-to-understand terms. They may nod their heads as they identify with your personal experiences. They may find your analogies helpful. But sooner or later they will want to have "proof"—quotes and evidence which show that your point is true on a broader scale. Two kinds of proof are *testimony* and *statistics*.

Testimony

A testimony is an expert's confirmation of your conclusion. Most audiences will consider your speech incomplete unless you substantiate your points with some sort of trustworthy opinion. Expert testimony can be used to *clarify* an argument or to *prove* it.

Five tips to make your quotes "stick" in the minds of the audience include:

1. Quote the source accurately, in the proper context, making it clear that the source is actually saying what you claim.

2. When possible, choose sources with which the audience is familiar. If this is not possible, briefly explain why the source should be believed.

3. If most authorities agree with the source you are quoting, say so. If most authorities disagree, explain why the source you are quoting, not the others, should be believed.

4. Find quotes that are short, to the point, and phrased in an interesting manner.

5. The best quotes come from a source you would not expect to take

> "Every man is said to have his peculiar ambition. Whether it be true or not, I can say for one that I have no other so great as that of being truly esteemed of my fellow men, by rendering myself worthy of their esteem. "
>
> —Abraham Lincoln, candidate for the Illinois state legislature at age 23

> "With malice toward none; with charity for all; with firmness in the right, as God gives us to see the right, let us strive on to finish the work we are in: to bind up the nation's wounds; to care for him who shall have borne the battle, and for his widow and his orphan, to do all which may achieve and cherish a just and lasting peace among ourselves, and with all nations."
>
> —Abraham Lincoln, second inaugural address, 1865

that position (e.g., an evolutionist testifying to evidence of a creator).

Where can you find good quotes? Top speakers keep copies of *Bartlett's Book of Quotations* or the *Oxford Dictionary of Quotations* on hand to reference tens of thousands of interesting quotes on a wide range of subjects. Magazine articles, Web sites, books, and personal interviews also can yield a rich supply of quotes. If you are speaking on a controversial issue such as abortion, check with a pro-life organization for quotes and statistics which they have found helpful in persuading people.

To use quotes properly, integrate them right into the flow of your speech as the following examples demonstrate:

• Christians often debate whether trying to get rich is a good or bad thing. Some argue that it is good to have money because you can do a lot of good things. Others believe that money is a corrupting influence. Actually, both perspectives miss the point. It is not whether money is good or bad, but whether you desire money so much that you actually become a slave to it. *As Jesus Christ said in Luke 16:13, "No servant can serve two masters. Either he will hate the one and love the other, or he will be devoted to the one and despise the other. You cannot serve both God and money."*

• All too many people are willing to forfeit their liberty in exchange for safety. This was not the case with our Founding Fathers; they were willing to risk everything in order to be free. As Patrick Henry said in his magnificent speech at St. John's Church in 1775, *"It is in vain, sir, to extenuate the matter. Gentlemen may cry, peace, peace—-but there is no peace. The war is actually begun....What is it that gentlemen wish? What would they have? Is life so dear, or peace so sweet, as to be purchased at the price of chains and slavery? Forbid it, Almighty God! I know not what course others may take; but as for me, give me liberty or give me death!"*

• Many leaders fail because they remain passive when action is imperative. Powerful leaders become powerful because they convey a sense of urgency. This is evidenced vividly in Martin Luther King's famous "I Have a Dream" speech: *"We have.... come to this hallowed spot to remind America of the fierce urgency of now ....Now is the time to make real the promises of democracy. Now is the time to rise from the dark and desolate valley of segregation to the sunlit path of racial justice....Now is the time to make justice a reality for all of God's children."*

Statistics

A statistic is a numerical summary of data which demonstrates that an individual case applies to a large population. If you tell a story about feeling lonely as a child, people feel sorry for you. If you give a statistic about the vast numbers of children who feel alone, people are more likely to see loneliness as a serious problem.

These five strategies for using statistics will bring your speech to life:

1. Use statistics in moderation. Overusing them creates confusion.

2. Round off whole numbers. Instead of saying "136,421" say "more than 135,000."

3. Use graphics and visual aids, if possible. Audiences understand numbers and percentages best when presented visually.

4. Use recent statistics, and briefly describe how they were gathered.

5. Give the source of the statistics, and reinforce the credibility of the source.

The more complex a statistic, the more care you must take to present it properly. If using visual aids is not possible, think of an analogy which makes a statistic relevant. For example, Christian pro-life speaker Steven Carr uses a statistic to illustrate that the earth does not have a problem with overpopulation. He notes the earth's billions of inhabitants, standing shoulder to shoulder, would take up about 20 billion square feet. Since there are 27,878,400 square feet in a mile, the entire population of the earth would fit

inside 718 square miles. He completes his case through an analogy by explaining that a crowd assembled this way would fit within the city limits of Jacksonville, Florida. This analogy takes a mind-boggling statistic and frames it in terms that we can understand.

Of course, anyone can arrange statistics to support a case which is invalid. As Charles H. Grosvenor said, "Figures won't lie, but liars will figure." So, when in doubt, leave it out.

Using the **S. T. E. P.** system in your speech may seem stiff and unnatural at first. Perhaps it may feel awkward to move methodically from one point to the next, but there is an easy solution to this problem, and that is what we will work on next.

Dancing Gracefully With Evidence

A practiced speaker creates thoughtful transitions between each point so the speech flows naturally. For example, a seguey from "state" to "translate" might look like this:

• [State] "I am concerned about the lack of sincerity in our cynical culture today.

• [Transition] But what does it really mean to be sincere?

• [Translate—Definition] The word 'sincere' means 'without wax.'

"Without the assistance of that Divine Being, who ever attended him, I cannot succeed. With that assistance I cannot fail. Trusting in Him, who can go with me, and remain with you and be everywhere for good, let us confidently hope that all will yet be well."

—Abraham Lincoln, farewell address at Springfield, Illinois before assuming the presidency

"I was early brought to the living reflection that there was nothing in the arms of this man, however there might be in others, to rely upon for such difficulties, and that without the direct assistance of the Almighty I was certain of failing. I sincerely wish that I was a more devoted man than I am. Sometimes in my difficulties I have been driven to the last resort to say God is still my only hope. It is still all the world to me."

—Abraham Lincoln

• [Translate—Explanation] In the ancient world unscrupulous merchants fixed broken pottery with wax and painted it to make it appear to be new and unbroken. To say that pottery was 'without wax' was to say that it was genuine; what you see is what you get."

Using this same speech example, here are some other transitions:

From TRANSLATE to EXEMPLIFY:

"But how can you live 'without wax' in our culture today, when it is common to exaggerate or lie in order to advance your own interests? Maybe an example from the life of _____ _____ will help make sense of it all..." (then share your chosen example).

From EXEMPLIFY to PROVE:

"The life of _____, sadly, is the exception to the rule. Yet Christians should follow his lead; sincerity is not optional. The Apostle Paul said in Romans 12:9, 'Love must be without hypocrisy. Detest evil; cling to what is good.'"

Write transitions as part of your outline and practice them until they become natural for you. The audience will appreciate the way you dance gracefully from point to point.

How the S. T. E. P. System Will Transform Your Public Presence

The **S. T. E. P.** system is more than just a way to organize a speech. It is a way of *thinking*. If you think in an orderly fashion in everyday life, others will perceive you as more intelligent. Your ability to think on your feet also will improve. Of course, you may not go through each part of the **S. T. E. P.** system with every point you make. But if you think through how to explain your views, give examples, and prove them, you will find yourself armed with greater reasoning ability.

S. T. E. P. comes in handy whenever you want to be persuasive, whether in speaking, writing reports, or holding press conferences.

Moving Your Audience to Action

Let's step back and look at the bigger picture for a moment. While **S. T. E. P.** helps you organize each point of your speech, the overall goal is to make your talk as a whole persuasive. How can you organize your entire speech to create dynamic impact?

The traditional organization system is, "Tell them what you're going to tell them, tell them, and tell them what you told them." This is wise advice, but not specific enough to be of particular use. What we need is a clear persuasion formula.

Earlier in this chapter, we pretended that you created a genius potion called Mind Booster. I claimed then that to get people to buy it you must go beyond the mere fact that it works. People won't desire the solution until they see their personal need for it. Furthermore, even if they believe they need it, they may have objections to using it. Finally, even if they see their need, believe that it will work and have no objections to it, they must still be given a way to act on their belief. To make your case effectively, then, you must employ the four-step formula of persuasion:

Need + Solution - Objections + Action Strategy = Persuasion

Let's take a look at each element of the equation in turn.

Step One: Show People Their Need

Showing people their *need* may seem obvious, but you would be surprised how many speakers blithely skip this step. Without understanding their need, people will *never* act because they won't know why they ought to. If you want to sell a sports drink, for example, you must first help your customers identify their thirst.

To sell Mind Booster, you must make people acutely aware of how much they need it. Remind them of how frustrating muddled thinking can be. Help them recall times when a little extra brain power would have led to

better grades, more business success, mastery of complex information, or greater opportunities in life.

When introducing a new product, market researchers think up as many needs as they can, test them to see which ones are most compelling, and then assemble their message based on the market's perceived needs. A steak restaurant really doesn't sell steak. It sells sizzle. That is, it sells the benefits of *eating* the steak.

Step Two: Demonstrate the Solution

Showing people their need without providing an adequate solution results only in a frustrated, angry audience. To sell Mind Booster you must demonstrate that it meets the needs you have identified. Here again, many would-be persuaders miss the boat. Beyond the data, people have to see how the solution would work for *them personally*. Yes, you would want doctors and other credible authorities to testify to the effectiveness of Mind Booster, but even more important is having lots of people tell stories of how it changed their lives. When folks see that other people *just like them* achieved the desired results, they sit up and pay attention.

Let me mention here what I think is the most persuasive evidence you can use: *your own personal story.* Prospective Mind Booster customers would want to hear of how you felt inferior growing up because you weren't as smart as other kids. They would want to know the opportunities you missed because

> "We shall not fail—if we stand firm, we shall not fail. Wise counsels may accelerate or mistakes delay it, but, sooner or later, the victory is sure to come."
>
> —Abraham Lincoln

"You can fool all the people some of the time, and some of the people all of the time, but you cannot fool all the people all of the time."

—Abraham Lincoln

the "gatekeepers" of society wanted people who were more intelligent and articulate. They would want to be inspired by the specific ways your life has changed since taking Mind Booster. They probably would be thrilled to hear of how you "got back" at your arch-enemy by outsmarting him or her, something you were unable to do before. Your personal story is the best evidence you can use, and this is the part I especially like: no one else can use it quite like you can.

Step Three: Overcome Objections to Action

Let's say you have moved your audience to the point where they clearly see the need for Mind Booster, and they honestly believe it will work. But what if there are side-effects? Or what if the effect of Mind Booster is temporary and overuse leads to death?

To overcome customers' objections you would need first to alleviate people's fears about safety, using scientific witnesses to demonstrate that the potion is safe and brings no long-term negative consequences. Second, you would overcome their fear of change by helping them envision how much better life would be after taking it—how being smarter would give them new energy, confidence, wealth, and creativity. Third, you would show them that, because of the mass market, the potion is affordable on virtually any budget (or that their new intelligence will result in greater opportunities for earning income).

Step Four: Create a Strategy for Action

Finally, after taking all of the above steps, you would need to give people a way to act immediately by purchasing your potion for themselves and their loved ones. The easier this is to do, the more orders you will receive. Develop a payment plan so that they do not need to come up with the money all at once. Offer a money-back guarantee so the offer is risk-free. Give incentives to those who act right away (free products, discounts, a newsletter, etc.). Allow people to call, write, fax, e-mail or order on-line. Make taking action easy!

Putting the Persuasion Formula Together

In the 1940s a communications researcher named Alan Monroe devised a dynamic way to arrange "the sequence of ideas which, by following the normal process of thinking, motivates the audience to respond to the speaker's purpose." Monroe's sequence involves five motivations: (1) Getting the audience's attention, (2) Making the audience aware of a need, (3) Offering a solution which satisfies that need, (4) Visualizing how the solution would help them, and (5) Giving a specific action the audience can take. Let's take a look at each of these steps in turn.

Motivation One: Getting Their Attention

"Attention" is a valuable commodity. With all of the competing demands in modern society, advertisers, politicians, and others struggle mightily to gain people's attention. When you ask someone for their attention, you are asking them to set aside all of their other concerns and listen to *you*. Do not take this lightly. In the video lesson we discussed several strategies for getting the attention of an audience. There is no need to review those steps here. Just keep in mind that the time you invest in designing a creative attention-getting device will be time well spent.

Motivation Two: The Need

Monroe believed that the need step should be developed in four ways. First, the speaker should state the specific problem. Second, the speaker should clearly describe the need, illustrating it vividly. Third, the speaker should expand on the need using examples and statistics, demonstrating that it is widespread. Fourth, the speaker should apply these examples to the audience, making them hunger for the solution.

According to speech theorist Leon Festinger, a speaker should try to create "cognitive dissonance," that is, a sense of the inconsistency between where an audience member *is* and where he or she knows would be better. Human beings, by nature, wish their actions to be consistent with their beliefs. Therefore, if you show audience members that their actions are not consistent with their values, they are likely to stick around to hear how to become consistent again.

Suppose, for example, you are giving a speech on time management. Your *attention device* could be a motivational story about a businessman who went from failure to success by managing time more effectively. In the need step, you clearly outline the problem of poor time management. Then you illustrate this need through examples of common time management problems people face. Next you show how the lack of time management is a serious problem, affecting many people. Finally, you want to make audience members aware of the difference between where they *are* and where they *ought to be*. You might review the problems that bad time management causes: guilt over not spending enough time with one's family, being less productive financially, or frustration at feeling out of control. Once your listeners identify with the frustration and guilt of poor time management, they will be more open to a solution which helps them move from where they are to where they ought to be.

Motivation Three: Satisfaction

If audience members truly understand their need, they will likely want a solution. In the satisfaction step you

> "The brave men, living and dead, who struggled here, have consecrated it, far above our poor power to add or detract. The world will little note, nor long remember what we say here, but it can never forget what they did here. It is for us the living, rather, to be dedicated here to the unfinished work which they who fought here have thus far so nobly advanced."
>
> —Abraham Lincoln
> Gettysburg Address, 1863

> "Those who deny freedom for others deserve it not for themselves."
>
> —Abraham Lincoln

(1) state clearly what you wish them to do, (2) explain how they should do it, (3) explain how this solution will meet their need, (4) give examples of success to show that your solution works, and (5) answer the objections the audience has to employing your solution.

In the time management example, you might (1) show them how using a personal digital assistant (PDA) will allow them to organize their activities more effectively, (2) give details on how to use such devices, (3) show how PDA technology can help solve specific time management problems, (4) offer a personal experience or a story about using a PDA, and (5) answer common objections such as, "It costs too much," "It takes too much time," or "I've tried it in the past, and it didn't work."

Motivation Four: Visualization

The term "visualization" has collected a lot of New Age baggage in our day, but the basic principle is very simple: create a picture of what the world would look like with your solution in place. Help the audience imagine how things would be better if they accepted your solution.

With time management, you could say, "Disciplining yourself to use a planning tool is difficult, but imagine the benefits once you learn. No more embarrassment over missed appointments. No more worrying whether you accomplished everything you were supposed to. And best of all, you'll accomplish more in less time so you have *more* time to do what you want."

Motivation Five: Action!

In the action step you relate the solution back to the audience's needs. Illustrate that if the audience *acts* on what they have learned, it will *fulfill* their basic needs for security, peace of mind, respect, status, and a sense of accomplishment.

The more specific the action, the more likely audience members will be to embrace it. To continue with our example of time management, you could suggest a specific brand of PDA and tell them where to get it. Or you could tell them about a Web site or computer program which makes planning easier.

The most effective speakers have something to offer *right then*: a book, an audio program, or a handout. A word of warning here: if you are effective at convincing the audience of their need, you will lose credibility if you do not offer a specific way for them to satisfy that need! Don't waste credibility on vague solutions.

Three Steps to Take Right Now

In the following pages you will find three valuable tools to help you review and apply what you learned in Chapter Three:

1. Personal Application.

Invest some time reflecting on this chapter by journaling answers to the five review questions.

2. Designing Arguments.

Use this exercise to practice deciding which type of evidence will work best in 14 hypothetical situations (you'll find the answers in the sidebar on page 84).

3. "Creating a Need" Speech Project.

Here is your opportunity to take the first steps toward developing a persuasion mindset by gaining practice presenting a need to an audience.

Your New, Persuasive Self

You now hold in your hands the organizational tools of professionals.

Using these strategies, you will be more effective at selling your ideas, at persuading people to change their beliefs, and at moving people from passivity to action. In the marketplace, you could sell products, convince others to invest in your business ideas, or ask your boss for a raise! As a citizen, you could persuade people to vote, enlist support for a political cause, or run for office. As a Christian, you could teach God's Word in an interesting fashion, share your faith more effectively, or take a stand against hollow and deceptive philosophies.

At the beginning of Chapter Three, we presented Nehemiah as an effective leader. As you pray and seek God's will, you will be able to use the tools of persuasion to become a Nehemiah and re-build our crumbling culture.

"It is not my nature, when I see a people borne down by the weight of their shackles—the oppression of tyranny—to make their life more bitter by heaping upon them greater burdens; but rather would I do all in my power to raise the yoke, than to add anything that would tend to crush them."

—Abraham Lincoln
Cincinnati, Ohio,
Februrary 1861

Personal Application

"As you take steps to organize your speech, you will gain respect. As you gain respect, you will gain influence."

—Jeff Myers

Here are some exercises and questions to expand your thinking about evidence and persuasion.

- List some of the reasons personal experience is a powerful form of evidence.

- Could the use of personal experience be abused by a speaker? How?

- How does it enhance your credibility as a speaker to cite an expert's opinion of your subject?

• Look over the quotes from Abraham Lincoln's speeches cited in the sidebars throughout this chapter. What makes them noteworthy? What were some of the strategies Lincoln used to persuade his audiences?

• Think of a speaker you have heard who did not organize his or her speech effectively. What impression did that give you of the speaker? Of the speaker's message?

"The leading rule for the lawyer, as for the man of every other calling, is diligence. Leave nothing for tomorrow which can be done today... Extemporaneous speaking should be practiced and cultivated...and yet there is not a more fatal error to young lawyers than relying too much on speech-making. If anyone, upon his rare powers of speaking, shall claim an exemption from the drudgery of the law, his case is a failure in advance."

—Abraham Lincoln
Notes on Lawyers

Designing Arguments

Recall the types of evidence we have discussed in this chapter (definition, explanation, personal experience, example, analogy, testimony, and statistic). On the line next to each point, write the type of evidence that would best convey that point to an audience (Hint: each type is used twice). Answers are in the sidebar on page 70.

_____1. You want to show the similarity between pro-abortion politics and pro-slavery politics in 1850.

_____2. You want to persuade someone that the Founding Fathers saw America as a Christian nation.

_____3. You want to classify the duck-billed platypus as a mammal.

_____4. You want to describe the components of the new computer program you have developed.

_____5. You want to persuade a customer to buy a car based on that model's history of reliability.

_____6. You want to introduce the concept of "soteriology" to a Sunday school class.

_____7. You want to tell an audience about how you developed a budget to improve your finances.

_____8. You want to illustrate how difficult it was to talk about your faith in a particular situation.

What kind of need should you talk about? Here are some possibilities:

- A problem you observe in your school, workplace, community, or nation.

- A political or social issue which concerns you.

- A product or invention that may be of interest to the audience.

- A lifestyle change that would help audience members live healthier, more fulfilled lives.

- An inspirational strategy that equips people to face certain challenges.

_____9. You want to show an audience how your town's new anti-smoking ordinance might affect different kinds of businesses.

_____10. You want to convey to an audience how successful the New York Yankees baseball team has been throughout its history.

_____11. You want to describe to a child how deep the water in the deep end of the swimming pool really is.

_____12. You want to demonstrate how new environmental regulations will affect the price of your products.

_____13. You want to clarify a comment you made in a previous meeting.

_____14. You want to show that great leaders view courage as an important virtue.

Transition Phrases:

• "What do I mean by 'X'? _Webster's Dictionary_ defines it as 'Y'."

• "Since you may not have been aware of this problem, let me explain it in more detail."

• "Have you ever felt like that? I have. One time..."

• "The point brought up by 'X' is one we should seriously consider."

• "'X' was not alone in dealing with this problem. According to 'Y' it is actually very widespread."

• "This is something we can probably all identify with. Have you ever..."

"Creating a Need" Speech Project

Answers to "Designing Arguments" exercise (on pages 68-69): 1=analogy, 2=testimony, 3=definition, 4=explanation, 5=statistic, 6=definition, 7=personal experience, 8=personal experience, 9=example, 10=statistic, 11=analogy, 12=example, 13=explanation, 14=testimony

After a lot of practice, organizing speeches persuasively will become second nature to you, almost a habit. Until then, it is wise to carefully plan out each speech, to write your points in an outline, and to plan transitions between major points. The purpose of this project is for you to research and prepare a five-minute speech in which you present a need to the audience by organizing your evidence according to the **S. T. E. P.** system. In later speeches you will have the opportunity to work on the solution to this need.

Here are some guidelines to follow as you prepare:

1. Select a speech topic that interests you. To use the S. T. E. P. system, you should choose topics about which you can convey relevant personal experiences.

2. Tie this speech in with your earlier biographical speech. This might mean you address a need your hero from the biographical speech faced or about which he or she offered some special insight. Use your previous research to your benefit.

3. Cite the full source for definitions and quotes. For example, "Thomas Sowell, in his book, Conquests and Cultures, said..."

4. Write out key parts of your speech. In particular, write your first 50 words, your main points, and your transition sentences word for word until you become accustomed to transitioning between points.

5. Make good use of your conclusion. It should summarize the speech and refer to your introduction.

In the following pages, you will find an outline for your speech, a sample "Creating a Need" speech, and several tips about using each kind of evidence. Once you have looked over these materials, create the outline for your own speech on a separate sheet of paper.

"Creating a Need" Speech Outline

1. ATTENTION STEP

A. Attention device. Plan your first 50 words carefully to gain the audience's attention. Effective attention devices include examples, stories, personal experiences, shocking statements, and dramatic interpretations.

B. Relate the purpose of the speech. Recount the subject of the speech to yourself and the audience by establishing a strong topic sentence: "The purpose of this speech is to _____ by _____."

2. NEED STEP

A. State the specific problem. Use definitions and explanations to convey the problem to your audience.

B. Describe the need. Use examples, personal experiences and analogies to describe the need.

C. Expand on the need. Use testimonies and statistics to show that the need is real.

D. Apply the need to your audience. Use any of the seven types of evidence to help the audience understand how the need affects their lives.

3. CONCLUSION

Focus your presentation to help the audience draw the conclusions you have in mind. Be certain to relate the conclusion to your introduction and to your topic sentence.

Sample Speech

"The Temptation of Incivility"

Some time ago I was driving in a nearby city, in moderately heavy traffic. Suddenly I noticed a middle-aged woman in a dark green economy car so close to my rear bumper that I thought she was going to run into me. I was driving at or above the posted speed limit, but it didn't matter to her. In my rear view mirror I saw her yelling at me, arranging her fingers into particular gestures that were less than complimentary.

I moved into the other lane as quickly as I could to get out of her way, and she zoomed past, yelling and gesturing, her face contorted with anger.

I don't think *I* was the problem; she had blown a fuse and was showering sparks of rage on all those nearby.

It wasn't just road rage. It was that this woman had given in to the temptation of incivility. In our short time together I want to discuss this temptation to incivility and give examples of how civility is melting away in America.

The problem we face, to be blunt, is that rudeness and disrespect have weakened the foundations of civil society.

"Civility" comes from the French word for citizen. Civilized people live in harmony with others. Since this is a value passed from parents to children, "civility" throughout history meant good breeding, politeness, or courtesy.

In the old days, civil people were civil not because others deserved it, but because people were *raised* to be civil. When civility is no longer valued, we stop respecting others and lose all sense of community. We become nothing more than a bunch of lonely, inconsiderate slobs sharing space.

ATTENTION STEP

Gain audience interest through personal experience.

Relate the purpose of the speech.

NEED STEP

State the specific problem, using definitions to convey it to the audience.

Describe the need to the audience.

Tip—As you read this speech, check these sidebars for comments about things that make it more interesting:

- Each section is tied to the next through smooth transitions; the audience doesn't even realize the speaker is moving from one step to the next.

- The personal story is a very common one with which the audience can readily identify.

- Civility is not just defined; the history of it is briefly explained.

- The statistics are used to build up the speaker's point without detracting from the message.

- The quote from a historical figure does not relate directly to the problem of incivility; rather, it enlarges the point, suggesting that civilization itself is at stake.

**Apply the
need to the
audience.**

CONCLUSION

**Provide a
focus and
help the au-
dience draw
conclusions.**

There are numerous examples of the lack of civility in our society. Television programs which demean elected officials, police officers, clergy, and other authority figures are one sort. Parents who allow their children to be disrespectful, and even defend their children when they are punished for mouthing off to teachers, are another. There is also passive incivility: Ignoring the clerk at the grocery store; people living next door to one another for years, never having met; speaking rudely to the teller at the bank...or the representative at the airline ticket counter...or wherever.

This problem is real. Several years ago scholar Stanley Rothman conducted a study of the portrayal of civic and religious authorities on television, concluding that the number of negative portrayals in the 1950s was extremely low. By 1990, the statistics had reversed. Disrespect had become a high art. With the average American watching 28 hours of television a week, children are learning to be more articulate and bold in their incivility.

Or maybe it is just that we Americans think so highly of ourselves that other people have become inconvenient. We have a right to be left alone, and anyone who dares enter our space uninvited should rightfully incur our wrath.

Years ago I read a book called *Democracy in America* by Alexis de Tocqueville. Among his many profound observations, de Tocqueville said the following:

> If the lights that guide us ever go out, they will fade little by little, as if of their own accord....We therefore should not console ourselves by thinking that the barbarians are still a long way off. Some peoples may let the torch be snatched from their hands, but others stamp it out themselves. (New York: Harper and Row, 1969, pp. 464-465)

Not all civilizations die through invasion. Some just...fade away. They lose the core truths that tie people together, and they lapse into silence. The cry of the populace is "leave me alone," and perhaps the ultimate hell is that this wish will be granted.

Let's not just point fingers at others, however. Incivility tempts us all. When was the last time you walked through your neighborhood and visited with folks? Do you even know your neighbors' names? For that matter, do you know the names of those who wait on you at the grocery store? At Wal-Mart? When was the last time you looked a stranger in the eye and said hello?

And what about our own families? How often do you have meals together? How often do you talk during those meals? How often do family members all watch television at the same time—in different rooms of the house? This is a far cry from even 50 years ago, when families commonly gathered in the parlor each evening to listen to the radio, play games, visit, and, as bizarre as it seems now, sing together.

Yes, it is quite clear that the temptation of incivility is one we all face. It is a real problem. We are all guilty.

Come to think of it, that is probably what bothered me most about the middle-aged woman in the dark green economy car. It wasn't just that she was lacking in civility. It was that I saw, in her, too much of myself.

- When the needs section is applied personally, the speaker asks questions rather than making accusations. The audience gets the point but without feeling defensive.

- The speaker chooses vivid words and phrasing to make the points more interesting.

REACH THE HEART OF YOUR AUDIENCE

(15 minutes)

Three things to know about your audience

1. **What are they** _____?

   • Race, religion, sex, occupation, political beliefs, geography, background, common interests

2. **Why are they** _____?

   • Do they meet regularly? What have they done in previous meetings?

3. **What** _____ **them into action?**

   • Unity, order, progress, success, reputation, money, power, adventure, beauty, acts of good will

Six Steps To Audience Impact

1. **What does the situation** _____ **of you?**

2. **What is the criteria for** _____?

3. **What are the three biggest** _____ **facing audience members?**

4. **What is the** _____ **of your message?**

5. **What would you like them to** _____ **or** _____?

6. **Can you state the** _____ **of your speech in one** _____?

Reach the Heart of Your Audience

Focus on Great Communicators:
Teddy Roosevelt

CHAPTER AT A GLANCE

- Moving from respect to belief.
- Your next few words can make history.
- Golden apples on a silver tray.
- What makes a great leader great?
- Keys to understanding an audience.
- Tapping into the audience's inner drives.
- Three things that trigger almost any audience to action.
- The ethics of audience analysis.
- Grace and truth lead to respect and belief.
- Three steps to take right now.

As HE WAS KNOWN BY A generation of Americans, "T. R." lived every moment to its fullest. "I don't think any President ever enjoyed himself more than I did," he said. Theodore Roosevelt's success as president came from the integrity and energy that he brought to every task. As a speaker, he was animated, persuasive, and long-winded. Once he escaped death at the hand of an assassin because the bullet was slowed by a thick speech manuscript in his breast pocket. Shaken, Roosevelt proceeded to deliver his lengthy address anyway.

> "...the man who really counts in the world is the doer, not the mere critic—the man who actually does the work, even if roughly and imperfectly, not the man who only talks or writes about how it ought to be done."
>
> —Theodore Roosevelt
> 1891

Roosevelt is still the youngest man to have ever held the office of president, attaining the presidency at age 42 after the assassination of William McKinley. His far-ranging reforms in industry and environmental conservation gained the admiration of conservatives and liberals alike. Roosevelt's "square deal" policy enabled poor Americans to earn a livable wage. He reduced government debt by 90 million dollars, built the Panama Canal, expanded the navy, passed consumer protection laws, regulated the railroads, and brought federal protection to 230 million acres of parks and forests.

Roosevelt is credited with expanding the power of the presidency through executive orders and with using his high office as a "bully pulpit" to bring attention to causes he considered important. He exhibited an astonishing ability to understand what people were thinking and to tap into those thoughts to garner support for his policies, truly a hallmark of a great communicator.

Speech communication isn't just about getting your point across. It's about reaching hearts and inspiring people toward lasting change. Teddy Roosevelt never rose to the lecturn to entertain people. He wanted them to be different—to be better than before. That's what it means to reach the heart of an audience.

Moving From Respect to Belief

What makes an audience want to believe you? Communication expert Bert Decker, in *You've Got to Be Believed to Be Heard,* explains that "[B]elief is emotionally based. It bypasses the intellect….It is perceived and felt rather than analyzed." In other words, for an audience to be persuaded, they must be emotionally convinced that you have their best interests at heart. Abraham Lincoln wrote:

> If you would win a man to your cause, first convince him that you are his sincere friend. Therein is a drop of honey that catches his heart, which is the high road to his reason, and which, when once gained, you will find but little trouble in convincing his judgement of the justice of your cause, if indeed that cause be a just one.

In the last chapter, you learned to organize speeches for maximum impact. Yet your logically organized speech only becomes persuasive when you connect, heart-to-heart, with your audience. Learning to reach the heart is the next step in becoming a great communicator.

To reach your audience at its core, you must know the hearts of the people to whom you speak and be able to see the world from their viewpoint. Only when they are convinced that you care will they allow you to persuade them. King Solomon recognized the importance of *understanding* before *persuading*. He wrote "A fool does not delight in understanding, but only wants to show off his opinions" (Proverbs 18:2) and "The one who gives an answer before he listens—this is foolishness and disgrace for him" (Proverbs 18:13).

In this chapter, you will learn:

• Ten questions you can ask so you'll know the audience like the back of your hand.

• How to tap into your audience's inner drives by understanding what motivates them.

• Three triggers that will motivate almost any audience to action.

• The fine line between persuasion and manipulation, and how to persuade an audience ethically.

• How to succeed as a group's speaker—before you even walk into the room—with our unique audience analysis worksheet.

You've already learned how to become a *respected* speaker. Now it is time to discover the secret to being *believed*.

Your Next Few Words Can Make History

The old man surveyed the multitude— hundreds of thousands of people— their murmurs blending to form one unintelligible, unforgettable voice. Today was his farewell address. Soon he would be gathered to his fathers. What does someone say at a time like that? How could a few words penetrate the thick skulls of more than two million stubborn, rebellious souls loved dearly by God?

"Joshua, it is time," called Caleb, his voice choked with emotion. His beloved commander was dying, and Caleb doubted the nation would survive without him.

Joshua stood and faced the people. Whispers of anticipation skittered across the sea of hearers like pebbles across smooth ground.

Joshua thought back to the stories of Abraham, Isaac, Jacob, Joseph. He recalled his mother's vivid description of the Red Sea parting. He recalled the years of wandering across barren desert. He remembered his awe as the walls of Jericho caved in. But these people had not been there. They did not understand.

"This is what the Lord, the God of Israel, says," Joshua began, his ancient voice strong. "'Long ago your ancestors, including Terah, the father of Abraham and Nahor, lived beyond the Euphrates River and worshiped other gods. But I took your father Abraham from the region beyond the Euphrates River, led him throughout the land of Canaan, and multiplied his descendants.'"

Joshua reminded the people about the awesome power of Yahweh and recalled for them God's provision of

> "I have a perfect horror of words that are not backed up by deeds."
>
> —Theodore Roosevelt
> Oyster Bay, NY
> 1915

> "A healthy-minded boy should feel hearty contempt for the coward and even more hearty indignation for the boy who bullies girls or small boys, or tortures animals.... What we have a right to expect of the American boy is that he shall turn out to be a good American man."
>
> —Theodore Roosevelt
> "The American Boy," *St. Nicholas Magazine,* 1900

manna and water in the desert. He warned them against false gods.

Certain now they had heard him, Joshua concluded: "Therefore, fear the Lord and worship Him in sincerity and truth. Get rid of the gods your ancestors worshiped beyond the Euphrates River and in Egypt, and worship the Lord. But if it doesn't please you to worship the Lord choose for yourselves today the one you will worship: the gods your fathers worshiped beyond the Euphrates River, or the gods of the Amorites in whose land you are living. As for me and my family, we will worship the Lord" (Joshua 24, selected verses).

Golden Apples on a Silver Tray

Joshua's farewell address was surely memorized and cherished by every hearer. His words, and the people's response, would determine the nation's future. But Joshua knew his audience—their experiences, their fears, and their history. Most importantly, he knew what moved them to action: a call to commitment, to choose the right course of action and to despise what was wrong.

It worked. In a growing crescendo, voices rose by the tens of thousands. "We too will worship the Lord, because He is our God!" And as long as the leaders who heard Joshua's farewell address were alive, the people followed the Lord (Joshua 24:31).

Joshua understood the significance of words. Proverbs 25:11 says, "A word spoken at the right time is like golden apples on a silver tray." When we speak, we must choose words carefully so their truth and value are easily recognized. This requires concentration, prayer, and a sensitivity to the hopes, dreams, and desires of others. The strategies that follow will show you how to reach the heart of *your* audience.

What Makes a Great Leader Great?

In August 1914, Sir Ernest Shackleton left England on the *Endurance* to explore the South Pole. The ship was crushed in the brutal ice floes of Antarctica, and Shackleton and his men drifted on an ice pack for five terrifying months. Throughout the ordeal, Shackleton exhibited extraordinary leadership in rallying his men to keep them alive. One man later said Shackleton was "the greatest leader that ever came on God's earth, bar none."

Shackleton was a great leader because he understood what motivated people to achieve great things. Preparing for the expedition, he placed an advertisement in the London newspapers. It read: "Men wanted for hazardous journey. Small wages, bitter cold, long months of complete darkness, constant danger, safe return doubtful. Honor and recognition in case of success." Five thousand men and two women applied for the 20 openings.

Shackleton understood that every person wants to have a reason to live that is so compelling, so consuming, it is worth dying for. This recognition cemented his reputation as the kind of leader everyone wants to follow when all hope seems lost.

As a public speaker, you have the opportunity to understand people, reach into their hearts, and draw out their very best. This chapter reinforces the principles introduced in the video lesson by discussing in detail how to match your presentation to an audience's needs so that you become truly persuasive.

Keys to Understanding an Audience

A great presentation begins long before the day of the speech—with a thorough analysis of the audience. When you understand the characteristics of your audience, you can better discern their motivations and values and how they might be persuaded to believe, value, or do what you are suggesting.

As I explained in the video session, the key to understanding the audience is to answer three questions:

• What are they like?

• Why are they meeting?

• What spurs them to action?

Let's look at each of these three questions in greater detail.

1. What is the audience like?

Are they business people? Stay-at-home moms? *Star Trek* fans? War veterans? Church members?

An entire industry has grown up around searching out statistical differences between people based on their defining characteristics. Companies that sell laundry detergent, for example, can tell you exactly who their target customers are (gender, age range, region of the country), reasons for the color and design of the box, what words on the box get people to buy their soap instead of another brand, when to run commercials and on what programs, approximately how many people will use coupons to purchase the product, and how much the coupons need to be worth to get people to choose their brand. Successful companies analyze every aspect of the market to learn as much as they can about their customers.

Obviously, speakers don't spend the amount of time analyzing their audience that market researchers do their targets. Yet few speakers succeed without analyzing their audience in some way. I vividly recall the day, while I was a student at Baylor University, President Ronald Reagan came to speak. He seemed to really *know* our school. He even led the audience in a school cheer, and the students went wild. It probably took Reagan's staff no more than five minutes to find out about Baylor, but we loved him for it.

Since you likely will not have access to statistical information about your

"A thorough knowledge of the Bible is worth more than a college education."

—Theodore Roosevelt

"It is not the critic who counts...the credit belongs to the man who is actually in the arena, whose face is marred by dust and sweat and blood, who strives valiantly, who errs and comes up short again and again, because there is no effort without error or shortcoming, but who knows the great enthusiasms, the great devotions, who spends himself for a worthy cause."

—Theodore Roosevelt
"Citizenship in a Republic,"
Speech at the Sorbonne,
Paris, 1910

audience, you will need to make some intelligent guesses. I have outlined below a list of ten questions about audience characteristics which tap into an audience's beliefs, attitudes, and values. Learn to ask them consistently, and you'll know the audience like the back of your hand.

• *Characteristic #1: What is their age range?* People from different generations hold different values, and these values shape how they take in information from a speaker. Older people tend to have more money, are more likely to have a strong work ethic, to know how to weather difficult circumstances, to trust the government to take care of problems, etc. Younger people also have certain general tendencies, such as a sense of personal autonomy and an entrepreneurial spirit.

• *Characteristic #2: How much do they make?* The potential differences between people at different income levels are too numerous to list. Those in wealthy neighborhoods tend to be of certain races and religions, have higher education levels, buy specific kinds of products, give money to particular causes, and vote for more conservative political candidates. People in middle class or poor areas also tend to have fairly well defined characteristics.

• *Characteristic #3: How many years of education have they attained?* The more years of education people have, the more likely they are to have a

higher income, vote for certain kinds of candidates, and live in certain neighborhoods. And, generally speaking, the more educated the members of the audience, the more critical they are of a speaker's message (they tend to *think* they know more about the subject).

• *Characteristic #4: Are they mostly men or women?* Men and women generally have different communication styles, and speakers must keep this in mind when speaking to groups which are primarily one gender. Quoting statistics about the significance of a problem might be persuasive to men, but women will also want to hear how it affects people individuallly.

• *Characteristic #5: Where are they from?* People's attitudes and lifestyles are often a product of where they live—the region of the nation as well as whether they live in the city, the suburbs, or in the country. In America, people from the South have a different cultural background than Northerners or Westerners. Westerners tend to be more independent and libertarian, comfortable with wide open spaces and individualistic lifestyles. Many Southerners stereotype Northerners as untrustworthy and condescending while many Northerners, on the other hand, stereotype Southerners as uneducated and bigoted. Whatever the reality of the situation, it would be unwise for a person from one part of the country to assume that everyone else is just like they are.

• *Characteristic #6: What do they do?* People in America tend to define themselves by their occupation more than any other factor. When two people meet, one of the first questions they ask each other is, "What do you do?" A person's occupation can cause them to see the world in a particular way, approving or disapproving of certain messages. Lawyer jokes to a group of attorneys would be inappropriate, for example, unless you are also a lawyer and are poking fun at yourself. Likewise, you must be careful how you critique the educational system in front of a group of teachers, or how you talk about unions to employees in an auto assembly plant.

• *Characteristic #7: How do they vote?* A person's political party affiliation strongly influences how they receive information. Differing political leanings lead people to very different philosophies of life. I once spoke to a group of Canadians about the conflict between worldviews. In the process, I made light of a socialist professor I had in college. Later I found out a significant proportion of the audience were members of their country's socialist party. Had I known that, I would have framed my critique more gently so as not to alienate my listeners.

• *Characteristic #8: What is their race or national origin?* Often people of different ethnic origins have values or customs which are based on unique cultural experiences. I once spoke at a church attended predominately by Chinese immigrants. Imagine my pleasant surprise as audience members nodded and smiled as I spoke. I, of course, took this as a sign of agreement, but I found out later that many people in the audience strongly disagreed with my message. When I explained to my hostess that the audience had seemed very receptive, she said, "Our people tend to nod and smile to indicate that they hear you and understand you, not always to communicate agreement." While you *do* want to have respect for different ethnic and racial backgrounds, beware of playing to stereotypes. It should go without saying that people are not all alike just because they are part of a particular ethnic group. At the same time, knowing the tendencies of the group may help you shape your message so it communicates more effectively.

• *Characteristic #9: What are their religious practices?* A Buddhist will hold different values than a Christian. Even among groups of Christians, beliefs vary widely, from liberal to conservative. Religion is an *a priori* concern. That is, people tend to automatically accept or reject certain messages because of their religious beliefs.

• *Characteristic #10: What do they have in common?* Sometimes the shared experiences of audience members affect how they view a speaker. I once spoke in a Florida town which had been destroyed by a hurricane a few years

"Let the watch-words of all our people be the old familiar watch-words of honesty, decency, fair-dealing, and common sense....We must treat each man on his worth and merits as a man. We must see that each is given a square deal, because he is entitled to no more and should receive no less."

—**Theodore Roosevelt**
New York State Fair, Syracuse, NY 1903

"There are good men and bad men of all nationalities, creeds and colors; and if this world of ours is ever to become what we hope some day it may become, it must be by the general recognition that the man's heart and soul, the man's worth and actions, determine his standing."

—Theodore Roosevelt
Letter
Oyster Bay, NY
September 1903

before. It obviously would have been unwise for me to use examples about hurricanes or attempt to give advice on how to survive difficult times. The memories were too fresh and bitter. Some things are better left alone.

As you reflect on the composition of an audience, put together a list of six or seven defining characteristics. Then, narrow them down to a statement which you feel describes the audience as a whole. Ask your host if it is accurate. Once you understand what—more than anything else—the members of this audience have in common, make that your "target" audience.

2. Why is the audience meeting?

I once spoke to an audience of Christian school teachers in another country. Since I regularly speak to such groups, I didn't invest much time analyzing the audience. This time, though, I was quite surprised when I found the listeners grim, unhappy and tense. I tried to be funny; they didn't laugh. I tried to be motivational; they would not be moved. I felt like a complete failure. Later I discovered that one of the reasons they were meeting was to resolve a serious internal conflict. The presence of certain individuals in the meeting caused others to be on-edge and unresponsive. Although this was not caused by my presentation, it certainly affected it. If I had taken time to research the audience, I might have approached the situation very differently.

Why an audience is gathered in the first place is one of the most significant things a speaker can consider. Is it a required event such as a class? Are people eager to learn, or are they just there to be seen by others? Are they hungry for information? If audience members are not motivated to be there, you will need to demonstrate *why* they ought to know the information you are presenting. If, on the other hand, audience members are highly motivated to listen, you can invest most of your speech time telling them what you want them to do.

A lack of audience analysis is the downfall of many otherwise good speeches. During the 1960s and 70s, the threat of nuclear war terrified many Americans. Helen Caldicott, a medical doctor, traveled the country trying to convince people of the seriousness of the nuclear crisis. Most of her speeches focused on the devastation nuclear war would cause on planet earth. She went into great detail about how many people would be killed, including the gruesome details of death by radiation. In addition, she relished watching audience members shiver as she vividly described how cockroaches would infest the planet, being one of the few creatures that could survive toxic doses of radiation. It was all very serious and grotesque, and her audiences quickly began to share her fear of nuclear weapons.

As Dr. Caldicott's message spread, awareness grew, and people wanted to know how to respond. But

Dr. Caldicott continued giving the same speech. Once, as she launched into her presentation, a man shouted, "We know all that. But what do we *do* about it?" Caldicott was unprepared to answer. Ironically, her messages became less popular, not because people disagreed, but because she had failed to analyze the changing needs of her audiences.

3. What triggers the audience to act?

It has been said that the most popular radio station in America is WIIFM: <u>W</u>hat's <u>I</u>n <u>I</u>t <u>F</u>or <u>M</u>e. Except in rare situations, people will not listen simply because you have something to say. You must convince them of how they will benefit from your message.

Good speakers are constantly aware of people's motives. A "motive" is that which sets a person into motion—an inner drive—and which causes a person to think and act a certain way. Some people act because they can gain financially. Others are uninterested in finances but are motivated by a love of knowledge, or adventure, or any number of things.

People rarely act contrary to their motives. A person motivated by security, for instance, is not likely to engage in a risky scheme. To be successful as a speaker, you must make wise guesses as to what motivates people and appeal to them based on those motives.

Imagine, for example, that you want to give a speech advocating an increase in government funding for job training. Imagine further that your audience consists of business people who are concerned about paying too much money in taxes. To suggest they support your policy "because it is the right thing to do" might motivate some people, but it would probably be even more effective if you could demonstrate that the new program could be funded without a tax increase and that the improved training of workers would benefit businesses in the community. That sort of shrewd planning can make the difference between persuading only a few people and persuading many.

Tapping Into the Audience's Inner Drives

It can be difficult to figure out why people do what they do, but by observing them for a period of time, you can make some fairly accurate guesses. A person who spends a great deal of time on his or her personal appearance is probably motivated to be seen by others as attractive. A person who works 80 hours a week is probably motivated by financial security or status. Good communicators observe people to figure out what is important to them.

Some time ago on a business trip to Washington, D. C., I had scheduled an early morning flight home. Arising much earlier than I usually do, I stumbled through my morning routine and

> "No man can lead a public career really worth leading, no man can act with rugged independence in serious crises, nor strike at great abuses, nor afford to make powerful and unscrupulous foes, if he is himself vulnerable in his private character."
>
> —Theodore Roosevelt
> *An Autobiography*
> 1913

> "There is not in all America a more dangerous trait than the deification of mere smartness unaccompanied by any sense of moral responsibility"
>
> —Theodore Roosevelt
> Abilene, KS
> 1903

pulled onto the highway before 5:00 a.m. As I merged into the traffic, I was shocked to find thousands of cars already jamming the roads into the city.

Maybe these early risers *had* to get up that early in order to make a living. But it is also possible, perhaps likely, that they were in pursuit of something more. Maybe they sought to prove their loyalty and competence by being the first to arrive at the office. Or maybe they were pursuing power. In any event, arriving at work early in the morning was a means to an end which revealed something about their motivations.

Desiring to have other people look up to us and think well of us is a powerful motivator. If you were to speak to an audience of those on the highway that morning you would probably need to appeal to their desire for status or draw their attention to the fact that this drive is sometimes unhealthy and offer remedies to alleviate the pressure in their lives.

Three Things That Trigger Almost Any Audience to Action

A motive is like a language. If you address a Spanish-speaking audience in English, you will not communicate effectively. Similarly, you will not reach an audience by communicating with them based on *your* motives rather than *theirs*.

Research shows that most people are motivated by three things. First, they are motived by a desire for *unity*—to have community with like-minded individuals. Second, they are motivated by a desire for *order*—they want their lives to make sense and to be protected from chaos. Third, they are motivated by a desire for *progress*—they want to grow richer in knowledge, expertise, money, and life experiences.

If you understand these three things about people, you will have tremendous persuasive power. They are "default" motivations—that is, even if you do not know much about your audience, you can assume the vast majority of people share them.

Here are some other powerful reasons people do what they do:

- Acceptance (popularity or respect)

- Adventure (an exciting and rewarding experience)

- Altruism (acting with others' best interests at heart)

- Attractiveness (appearance to members of the opposite sex)

- Freedom from restraint (the liberty to do as they wish, such as make beneficial economic and social choices)

- Security (self-preservation, financial well-being)

You can probably think of others. The point is that when you understand people's motives, you'll have insight into what they think is important.

The Ethics of Audience Analysis

Many people are motivated to understand their audiences so they can manipulate them into doing wrong. Obviously, this is unethical. There is another kind of unethical persuasion: avoiding the truth by telling the audience only what you think they want to hear. Many politicians earn a reputation as "shifty" because they say one thing to one group and the opposite to another. They try to please everyone and are thus mistrusted by all.

In the Bible, the book of Daniel provides a good example of ethical audience analysis. Daniel and his friends had been taken captive and placed into the service of King Nebuchadnezzar. While the men were learning the language and literature of the Babylonians, the king insisted they eat food from his own menu. Daniel and his friends considered the king's food to be defiled because a portion of it had been offered to idols. Because they were captives, however, they could not risk making the king angry. What should they do?

Daniel first determined the king's motives. Likely, the king was more concerned with having healthy and smart servants than he was with exactly what they ate. So Daniel approached the king's steward with a proposal: "Please test your servants for 10 days.

Let us be given vegetables to eat and water to drink. Then examine our appearance and the appearance of the men who are eating the king's food" (Daniel 1:12-13). After ten days, Daniel and his friends looked so much healthier that the king's steward changed *all* of the young men's diets.

Daniel did not base his appeal on the desire to avoid defiling himself. Rather, he wisely appealed to the steward based on what was important to the king. The Bible abounds with examples of similar approaches. God understands that to persuade people we must attract them based on what is important to *them*, not to *us*.

Still, what about those situations in which you are tempted to hedge the truth in order to persuade the audience? Are there guidelines you can follow to be certain you are acting ethically? Here are some I recommend:

1. It is wrong to treat an audience as a means to an end.

I once heard a speaker frighten the audience into thinking civilization was on the verge of collapse. Once audience members were sufficiently frightened, he pressed them to invest in a questionable commodity which, in my judgement, would provide neither security nor alleviate the fears he had raised. Such persuasion is highly unethical. The speaker was merely enriching himself at the expense of the audience.

> "If a man does not have an ideal and try to live up to it, then he becomes a mean, base and sordid creature, no matter how successful."
>
> – Letter to his son Kermit, quoted in *Theodore Roosevelt* by Joseph Bucklin Bishop, 1915

"Criticism is necessary and useful; it is often indispensable; but it can never take the place of action, or be even a poor substitute for it. The function of the mere critic is of very subordinate usefulness. It is the doer of deeds who actually counts in the battle for life, and not the man who looks on and says how the fight ought to be fought, without himself sharing the stress and the danger."

—Theodore Roosevelt
1894

2. It is wrong to pressure someone into a decision they do not want to make.

If you "won't take no for an answer," you are probably acting unethically. I once was cornered by a promoter of a particular multilevel marketing organization, and regardless of how many times I said no, this person continued to badger me. Although I felt I was making my lack of interest clear, this person seemed not to notice. At the very least, he was being insensitive. Pushed to an extreme, such behavior can also be considered unethical.

3. It is wrong to use force to achieve your goals.

Using physical force to persuade someone is not really persuasion at all. Neither is the use of emotional or mental force. Wearing people down, forcing them to make a decision "right now," using peer pressure, or questioning a their character because they won't act as you suggest are all unethical. To suggest that a person is stupid or lazy because they don't respond is highly unethical.

4. It is wrong to threaten people.

When my first child was born, I received some information from a company selling a special monitor that would sound an alarm if the baby stopped breathing. The literature asked the question, "How will you feel if you haven't done everything you can to protect your child?" In essence, the company was suggesting that I would be guilty of neglect if I failed to buy their product. This is unethical persuasion.

5. It is wrong to obscure the truth.

A communicator who leaves out important details or buries them in "fine print" is acting unethically. Some time ago a friend told me he had fallen for a sales pitch in which he would receive a "free" vacation. The brochure showed pictures of a beautiful resort and gave the impression that this is where he would be staying. When he arrived, he was assigned to a seedy, run-down motel and then given a high pressure "tour" of the beautiful resort. The truth was there, but it was buried in several long paragraphs of fine print. The resort did their best to obscure the truth by the way they constructed their brochure. Christians are not to be involved in this kind of deception.

I hope these guidelines will make ethical persuasion easier to achieve. Being ethical is good business—those who play fair, win. In the end, ethical persuasion is simply the right thing to do, whether or not we ever benefit.

Grace and Truth Lead to Respect and Belief

The most respected public speakers are those who refuse to compromise their message, but who graciously take into account the fact that reasonable people disagree about some things. The Apostle Paul wrote in Colossians 4:6: "Your speech should always be gracious, seasoned with salt, so that you may know how you should answer each person." When people see you are full of grace but without compromise, *respect* quickly turns into *belief*. Gracious speech is beautiful, valuable and *rare*. Those who master it have a great influence for truth and righteousness in the world.

Three Steps to Take Right Now

As we reach the end of this chapter, you have a lot of shiny new tools for your public speaking tool box. You know how to understand an audience's characteristics, how to tap into their inner drives, and how to persuade them ethically. The remaining pages will expand on this theme in the following ways:

1. **Personal Application.** Invest some time reflecting on Chapter Four by journaling answers to the three personal application exercises.

2. **Audience Analysis Worksheet.** Go over this exhaustive list of questions with the host of your speech, and you can be confident you know your audience before you even walk in the door!

3. **"Offering a Solution" Speech Project.** In the speech project for Chapter Three you practiced presenting a compelling need to an audience. In this chapter's project, you will add a solution step based on your understanding of the audience. Once completed, this speech will be ready for presentation to a wide variety of audiences. The only remaining step will be developing delivery skills, and we'll get to that in Chapter Five.

> "Let us speak courteously, deal fairly, and keep ourselves armed and ready."
>
> —Theodore Roosevelt
> San Francisco, CA
> May 13, 1903

> "Eighty-five percent of audience members cannot remember the main point of a speech immediately after hearing it."
>
> —Jeff Myers

Personal Application

1. List three reasons why is it important for a speaker to understand the audience.

2. Besides Joshua or Daniel, think of one biblical character who understood his or her audience. Explain what leads you to this conclusion.

3. Assume that you are to deliver a speech persuading people to vote for a conservative candidate for Congress. Your audience consists of the following: Unionized factory workers, most of whom are between the ages of 25 and 40. The average wage is about $35,000 per year. Over 80% are Anglo, 10% are African-American and the rest are Asian-American or Native American. About 40% of the audience claims to be born-again Christians. Of the rest, about half attend church at least once a month. List as many things as you can think of which probably characterize the audience and explain how this will affect the way you present your information.

Audience Analysis Worksheet

Use the following worksheet to research and understand the audience to which you will be speaking.

Name of the group_____

Location _____

Date and time _____

Host _____

Mailing Address_____

City _____ State _____ Zip Code _____

Telephone _____ Fax _____

E-mail _____ Emergency number _____

Topic title _____

Topic description: The purpose of this speech is to_____

_____by _____

Audience demographic data:

- What races are represented?

- What are the main religious influences?

- What percentage are male and female?

- What occupations are represented?

- What political beliefs do they hold in common?

- What is distinctive about the history and the people of this area?

- What interests do they have in common?

> "Do what you can with what you have, where you are."
>
> —Theodore Roosevelt

Group distinctives:

• Which demographic characteristics best explain what the group is like?

• What is the group's purpose?

• How often does the group meet?

• What is the purpose of the group's meetings?

• What has the group done in previous meetings?

Motivations:

• What spurs group members into action?

• What do members hope to gain from the meeting?

• What are some of the audience's major concerns?

• What are the top three issues audience members face?

Criteria for success:

• What has to happen for my speech to be successful?

• Who are some of the group's previous speakers you considered successful?

• What did those speakers do that allowed them to succeed?

• Are there any political, social, or religious issues that are best to avoid?

• Are there any topics which are particularly sensitive and which should be avoided?

"Offering a Solution" Speech Project

This speech project prepares you to offer a compelling solution to a problem. You have already done part of the work in your biographical and evidence speeches. Now, combine those insights, and show the audience how they can act on what you have presented.

The purpose of this exercise is to research and prepare a well-organized 7-10 minute talk which presents a solution to a problem with which the audience members can identify. Here are some guidelines to follow:

1. **Select a speech topic that interests you. You will probably do well to expand on the same topic you chose for your need speech. For best results, incorporate the examples and ideas you learned from the hero of history you studied in the biographical speech.**

2. **Use the S. T. E. P. system. Even if you do not go through each step in every segment of your speech, you should be prepared to select the evidence which best proves each point.**

3. **Write out key parts of the speech, word for word, including the first 50 words, your main point, and transition sentences.**

4. **Use your audience analysis worksheet. As you present the solution, relate it clearly to your audience, using what you have learned from your pre-speech analysis.**

5. **Offer a realistic means of action. Remember, if individuals in the audience are persuaded by your presentation, they will want to act on what you say. Give them practical strategies for doing so.**

In the following pages you will find an outline for your speech, a sample solution speech, and additional tips about how to make your speech as persuasive as possible. Review these materials, and then create the outline for your own speech on a separate sheet of paper.

"Offering a Solution" Speech Outline

PLANNING TIP

The **S.T.E.P.** system organizes seven types of evidence:

S=STATE

T=TRANSLATE

Definition—To clarify a point.

Explanation—To expand a point.

E=EXEMPLIFY

Personal experience—When the point benefits from your example.

Example—When the point can benefit from another's experience.

Analogy—Illustrates a complex idea.

P=PROVE

Testimony—When the point needs backing from an expert.

Statistic—To show that something is important to a lot of people.

1. ATTENTION STEP

A. Plan your attention device.

- Plan your first 50 words, and capture the audience's attention.

B. Relate the purpose of the speech.

- Establish a strong topic sentence: "The purpose of this speech is to _____

by _____."

2. NEED STEP

A. State the specific problem.

- Use definitions and explanations to convey the problem to the audience.

B. Describe the need.

- Use examples, personal experiences, and analogies to describe the need to the audience.

C. Expand on the need.

- Use testimonies and statistics to show that the need is real.

D. Apply the need to the audience.

- Help the audience understand how the need affects their lives.

3. SOLUTION STEP

A. State what you want the audience to do.

B. Explain your solution. Use examples and analogies to clarify the steps you want the audience to take.

C. Show how the solution meets the need. Use testimonies and statistics to show how the solution will actually work.

D. Visualize the solution working. Use evidence which creates a picture of how taking action can be successful.

E. Answer objections. Think of reasons someone would not want to act, and answer those objections.

4. CONCLUSION

A. Reinforce the solution. Give the audience a succinct way to remember what to do.

B. Offer direction. Give audience members something practical do to—a handout with key points or some other tool which will allow them to act on the solution.

PLANNING TIP

Why are people motivated to do what they do?

Keep in mind the following as you answer that question: accomplishment, admiration, adventure, beauty, duty, friendship, God's will, good will, happiness, intelligence, legacy, love, meaning, order, peace, physical health, predictability, productivity, progress, prosperity, respect, security, status, truth, unity.

Sample Speech

There are ten common reasons people fail to act on what you say. You'll need to address these in order to persuade your audience to act:

1. They have unanswered questions.

2. They don't like you personally.

3. They don't see the need to act.

4. Their desire is not strong enough.

5. They don't perceive how they would benefit.

6. Other people are not taking action.

7. They don't feel they have the time, money or energy.

8. They think you are wrong.

9. They disagree with your conclusions.

10. They fear change.

ATTENTION STEP

Attention device

Relate the purpose of the speech

NEED STEP

State the specific problem

Describe the need

Expand on the need

I once heard of a church where members thought it was against God's will to vote. They prayed that the right person would win, but they themselves refused to participate. In one election, there was a choice between two candidates: one was good and moral, the other shifty and unscrupulous. Concerned, 50 members of the church gathered for an all-night prayer vigil, but in the morning, they refused to vote. The good candidate lost by 35 votes.

I recognize that this is an extreme example, but it draws attention to an extreme problem. While people complain more and more about electing good candidates, the level of participation in elections is actually going down. In this speech I want to convince you that failing to vote is a serious problem and challenge you to get involved in the political process.

The problem can be stated quite simply: when people do not vote, our very system of government is in danger. Benjamin Franklin, upon emerging from the constitutional convention, was asked by a bystander, "Mr. Franklin, what sort of government have you given us?" Franklin replied, "A republic, madam, if you can keep it."

In a Republic, individual citizens select representatives who then cast votes as a representative body. If individual citizens do not vote, they lose the opportunity to express their opinions. The representatives begin to express their *own* interests or the interests of those who are willing to pay them money and attention. When Franklin and the other Founding Fathers established a republic, they understood that if people became apathetic toward their government, it would soon perish.

We in America—especially America's youth—need to take this citizenship responsibility seriously. In 1971, young people were for the first time guaranteed the constitutional right to vote. The 26th amendment to the United States Constitution says, "The right of citizens of the United States, who are eighteen years of age or older, to vote shall not be denied or abridged by the United States or by any State on account of age."

While young people have the constitutional right to participate, few actually do. According to statistics generated by the

Voter News Service, people between the ages of 18 and 32 vote in lower numbers than any other generation. They account for 1/3 of *eligible* voters, but less than 25% of the *actual* voters.

Apparently, young voters are expressing their views by staying away from the polls. Trust in government and interest in civic concerns are at an all-time low among America's young people. Thus begins an ironic downward spiral:

Because they aren't interested, they don't vote.

Because they don't vote, their interests are not represented.

Because their interests are not represented, young people have no voice.

Because young people have no voice, they lose interest and trust.

And on and on it goes.

One former young employee of Project Vote Smart put it this way: "By refusing to participate in the voting process, we are blindly turning over complete control on these issues to institutions we don't trust to make decisions in our own best interests."

Several years ago I taught a political communication course at a Christian college. I assumed that because political activism was the central theme of the class, students would take their citizenship responsibilities seriously. The day after the election, I discovered to my horror that only two of the students had actually voted and that most of them weren't even *registered* to vote. Yet they had complained day after day in class about the lack of Christian influence in government.

Okay, truth time. How many of you have ever criticized or expressed mistrust of a public official? Please raise your hand (don't be shy, we all do it). If you raised your hand, you join the vast majority of people I know who wish things were different. It is easy to talk about what "other people" have done or not done, but let's make it more personal. How involved are *you*? How are *you* exercising your responsibilities as a citizen?

The solution to this problem is quite simple. I want you to register to vote. Once you are registered, I want you to participate as a citizen by exercising your right to vote.

Registering to vote is easy. Forms are available at the driver's license bureau, the court house, and at any government office building. Most states now allow you to apply for voter registration on-line, and all states are required to allow you to register

---

Apply the need to the audience

SOLUTION STEP

State what you want the audience to do

Explain your solution

PLANNING TIP

Strategies for creating a compelling vision of the future:

1. Refer to the introduction of your speech and show how things would be different with your solution in place.

2. Ask the audience to imagine how your solution would help them achieve their goals.

3. Create a mental picture of a desired state, and describe it to the audience.

Show how the solution meets the need

Visualize the solution working

Answer objections

PLANNING TIPS

(1) Be clear about how the solution you offer answers the need you have presented!

If the audience believes the need exists, they will be frustrated with an inadequate solution. If your solution step cannot fully answer the need, then go back and rework the Need Step to make it more realistic.

(2) Effective quotes are short, sweet, and to the point. Good quotes should

• State the point eloquently or in a catchy way and

• Cement the point in people's minds. Refrain from using quotes that employ complex language or which are difficult to remember. Instead, explain those concepts using examples and analogies.

when getting your driver's license. Once you are registered, just watch the newspaper to find out when elections are held and where to vote. If you will be away, you can vote by absentee ballot. These may be ordered on-line or through a simple phone call to your local voter registration office.

After the disastrous incident of students at my college not voting, some colleagues and I decided to take voter registration more seriously. Using Internet technology, announcements, a poster campaign, and chapel speeches, we emphasized the importance of participation. Happily, almost 100% of the students registered to vote, and actual participation was about 80%, about four times the level of involvement of most college students. We realized that we *can* make a difference by encouraging people to do the right thing.

Imagine the incredible changes that could result if good people would go to the polls. If the 80 million Christians in America began to exercise their right to vote in large numbers, no election would be even close. Pro-family, pro-morality candidates could be elected to the school board, the city council, state legislatures, governorships, Congress, and even the presidency. It wouldn't be that hard to completely transform this nation. All it takes is one vote…by a concerned citizen…times millions of concerned citizens.

Now, you may be saying, "This all sounds great, but it can't be that easy. It is hard to register to vote." Or, "Christians shouldn't get involved in such a dirty business." Or, you might even be discouraged, saying, "My little vote won't make a difference."

Let me deal with each of these objections in turn. First, the difficulty of voter registration. It is not hard to do at all. In fact, I have enough voter registration forms for everyone in the audience. If you fill them out, I'll take them down to the courthouse for you, and you will receive your voter registration card in the mail. It's that easy.

Next, what about Christians getting involved in politics? I would suggest that politics in and of itself is not a dirty business. It gets dirty because good people fail to get involved. In Matthew 28:18 Jesus said, "All authority in heaven and earth has been given to me." Jesus has authority over all areas of life, including politics. William L. Fisher of the Christian Coalition suggests that Jesus' authority gives us the right to "ask Christians to do their part to bring Christian values to the shaping of public policy."

On the issue of whether one vote makes a difference, consider the following: In 1800, one vote gave Thomas Jefferson the presidency over Aaron Burr. In 1868, one vote saved Andrew Johnson's presidency. In 1960, 1 vote per precinct gave JFK the presidency. One vote does make a difference. That vote could be yours.

Dr. Terry Moffitt, a political consultant, says, "If you don't vote, you are irrelevant. You lose your right to complain." It is especially important for good people.

Right now I am handing out the voter registration forms. If you are already registered, just write your name, street address and e-mail address, and put "already registered." I'll contact you with information on the next election in your area and where you will need to go to vote. It will only take 30 seconds to do this, but it may be the most important 30 seconds you ever invest.

In conclusion, when Abraham Lincoln gave the *Gettysburg Address*, he strongly resolved that "government of the people, by the people, and for the people, shall not perish from the earth." Hundreds of thousands of men and women have died to protect your right to vote. Do not let their deaths be in vain.

CONCLUSION

Reinforce
the solution

Offer
direction

PLANNING TIP

Know precisely what you want the audience to do, value, or believe by the end of your speech, and make a point of asking them to do it. Good sentiment is not as important as good results.

DELIVER YOUR TALK WITH CONFIDENCE

(24 minutes)

The three most important delivery skills:

1. Visual _____

2. Physical _____

3. Vocal _____

Visual _____
Don't:

1. Avoid _____.

2. Writing your speech _____ for _____.

3. _____ your speech.

But do:

1. Look for _____.

2. Look at as many _____ as possible.

3. Gauge _____.

Physical Energy
Don't:

1. _____ the audience.

2. Use _____ movements.

But do:

1. Throw your _____ into the audience.

2. Use _____ to communicate _____.

3. Use _____ expressions to give the audience _____.

Vocal Enthusiasm
Don't:

1. Use vocal _____.

2. Use a _____ voice.

3. Use bad _____.

But do:

1. Speak with _____.

2. Vary your _____

3. _____ yourself.

4. Speak with _____.

5. Use _____ effectively.

Deliver Your Talk with Confidence

Focus on Great Communicators:
Patrick Henry

CHAPTER AT A GLANCE

- The next level: Masterful speaking.
- So your speeches aren't that great—welcome to the St. Paul Speech Club!
- Passion conquers fear and allows you to deliver your message with confidence.
- Delivery skills make your message irresistable.
- Visual directness: Connecting with your audience.
- Physical energy: Bringing the audience to life.
- Vocal enthusiasm: Keeping the audience interested.
- Delivery skills help you in everyday life.
- The most important delivery skill of all.
- Three steps to take right now.

"IS LIFE SO DEAR OR PEACE SO SWEET as to be purchased at the price of chains and slavery? Forbid it, Almighty God! I know not what course others may take, but as for me, give me liberty, or give me death!" These words proclaimed at St. John's Church in 1775 thrust the state of Virginia into the American War for Independence and paved the way for the speaker, Patrick Henry, to become known as the "Voice of the Revolution."

I cited Patrick Henry in the introduction to this study because there is no doubt he was one of America's greatest communicators. During the Continental Congress, Silas Deane of Connecticut wrote in a letter, "Mr. Henry…is the completest speaker I ever heard…in a letter I can give you no

> "Will the abandonment of your most sacred rights tend to the security of your liberty? Liberty—the greatest of all earthly blessings—gives us that precious jewel, and you may take everything else."
>
> – Patrick Henry
> Virginia Constitutional Convention
> June, 1788

idea of the music of his voice, or the high wrought yet natural elegance of his style and manner."

Henry's oratorical gifts became obvious when, as a lawyer of age 27, he spoke in the case of the Parson's Cause against taxation without representation. Two years later, Henry gave his second-most famous speech, against the stamp tax. Accused of treason, Henry replied, "If this be treason, make the most of it."

The father of 17 children, Henry was a devoted family man, businessman, and lawyer. He was the first governor of Virginia, serving five terms, and a driving force behind the inclusion of a bill of rights in the U.S. Constitution. Henry's courage and skill helped guide the young nation through its difficult first days, and his willingness to serve wherever needed demonstrated his commitment to the cause of liberty.

Patrick Henry's life demonstrates not only the impact of words but the power of God in using ordinary people to make an extraordinary difference in the world.

The Next Level: Masterful Speaking

I still remember the first time I observed a truly masterful speaker. He was brilliant, funny, and fascinating. He made me laugh and think at the same time. His jokes were hilarious but always tied to the point he was making. He strode up and down the aisles with complete confidence. He looked people in the eye and seemed to have control over the entire room. He used vocal variety with great effectiveness. Time passed so quickly that when he ended his address, I looked at my watch and was stunned to see he had spoken for 45 minutes. I wanted him to keep going.

I have now seen this speaker many times, and he never fails to get a standing ovation. Whether he is speaking to thousands of people or just a few dozen, his skill is apparent to all.

You may never be that good a speaker. And for that matter, *I* may never be that good a speaker. But the very skills this man used to communicate so well are available to all of us if we are willing to cultivate them.

This man exemplifies what are called "delivery skills" because they help a speaker make his or her message irresistible to the audience. So far in this coaching system you have been equipped with strategies to overcome fear, to organize your speech persuasively, and to reach the heart of the audience. What remains is to hone your use of visual directness, physical energy, and vocal enthusiasm.

Most speech instructors teach delivery skills at the beginning of their course, but here's why I don't: It is difficult to deliver a speech effectively until you really care about it and have confidently delivered it several times. Working on delivery skills only makes sense once you have something worth delivering.

In this chapter, you will learn:

• How to master the three delivery skills that can make your speech irresistible.

• How to connect with the audience using your eyes.

• How to transform nervous energy into enthusiasm.

• Three techniques for making your voice more interesting.

You'll also learn to use the power of passion, to speak boldly, make a positive first impression, and communicate better in everyday situations.

So Your Speeches Aren't That Great— Welcome to the St. Paul Speech Club!

The Apostle Paul was a terrible speaker by the standards of his day. Other speakers charged great sums of money; Paul charged nothing (his critics suggested that he *couldn't* charge money because his speeches were worthless). Other speakers were highly concerned with being eloquent while Paul's speeches were straightforward and unimpressive. Other speakers were cocky; Paul spoke "in weakness, in fear, and in much trembling" (1 Corinthians 2:3).

Yet Paul's preaching altered history. His words prompted the spread of the gospel of Jesus Christ all over the known world.

The lesson we learn from Paul is perhaps the most important of this coach-

ing system. Maybe you dread public speaking—you doubt that your message is important. Or maybe you are self-assured, convinced that you could persuade anybody of anything! Most of us are somewhere in between. But if we believe our gifts (or the lack thereof) are the main thing, we are wrong.

Paul's message changed the world not because he was a great speaker but because he spoke the truth passionately and with the power of God. "My speech and my proclamation were not with persuasive words of wisdom," he declared, "but with a demonstration of the Spirit and power, so that your faith might not based on men's wisdom, but on God's power" (1 Corinthians 2:4-5).

Nowhere was this more evident than in Paul's speech to the religious leaders of Athens. The book of Acts, chapter 17, says Paul's visit to Athens provided him the opportunity to influence many people. Proclaiming the resurrection of Christ, he debated the religious authorities in the synagogue. He walked through the markets and struck up conversations with merchants.

When the religious council of Athens got word of Paul's strange beliefs, they asked for an explanation. The pressure must have been tremendous; in Paul's day delivering a poor speech was seen as a character defect. Yet in the end, Paul's "Mars Hill Speech" exemplifies how a self-confessed poor speaker could rise to the occasion, in God's power, to deliver a commanding speech.

"All men are created free and equal. I have sworn upon the altar of God eternal hostility against every form of tyranny over the mind of man."

—Patrick Henry

"Whether this will prove a blessing or a curse, will depend upon the use our people will make of the blessings which a gracious God hath bestowed on us. If they are wise, they will be great and happy. If they are of a contrary character, they will be miserable. Righteousness alone can exalt them as a nation. Reader! Whoever thou art, remember this: and in thy sphere practice virtue thyself, and encourage it in others."

– Patrick Henry
1765

Paul began by saying, "I see that you are extremely religious in every respect," a compliment to their religious knowledge. He then described his encounter with a statue to an unknown god, announcing: "Therefore, what you worship in ignorance, this I proclaim to you." With that as his introduction, Paul presented the gospel powerfully and persuasively. He knew his audience. He understood their motives. He reached right past his fear and massaged his message into their hearts.

Did he succeed? Well, quite honestly, Paul's speech received a mixed response. Some in the audience sneered. Others were intrigued, wanting to hear more later, but only a few actually believed.

Like Paul, we are called to do our best. God does not call us to *perfection* but to *excellence*. He does not call us to *success* but to *obedience*.

Ultimately, your confidence as a communicator will not come from how good a speaker you are but from the truth of your message. "Delivery skills" without content accomplish nothing. Yet truth delivered with power is world-changing. That is the kind of great communication to which we aspire.

Passion Conquers Fear and Allows You to Deliver Your Message With Confidence

It was Christianity's biggest publicity nightmare—a trial which put biblical truth on the witness stand and forever changed the way Americans view Scripture, creation, and evolution.

The year was 1925. The newly formed American Civil Liberties Union, eager to gain public attention, decided to challenge the constitutionality of a Tennessee law which forbade teaching any theory of origins which contradicted the biblical account of Genesis.

The ACLU placed advertisements in Tennessee newspapers, looking for a teacher who would be willing to break the law in order to force the issue to trial, where it could be challenged before the whole world.

The citizens of tiny Dayton, Tennessee saw the challenge as an opportunity to gain national attention. They persuaded a physical education teacher named John Scopes to read, in violation of the law, a section of *Hunter's Biology* to a student. Thus began what is known as the "Scopes Monkey Trial."

Organizers appealed to William Jennings Bryan, former secretary of state and three-time democratic presidential candidate to represent the state against Scopes. Clarence Darrow, the crusty, controversial criminal defense lawyer secured John Scopes' agreement that Darrow be the lead defense attorney.

Bryan was perhaps the most famous speaker of his day. His words were precise and hard-hitting and his delivery skills formidable. Yet Bryan must have known the futility of his cause in the Scopes Trial. The world would be watching, and the press was uniformly scornful of his views. However, he pressed on. "Causes stir the world," he said, "and this cause has stirred the world."

In the end, Scopes was convicted of violating the law, but the negative publicity caused a massive defection of Christians from the public square. Religion became a private concern rather than a public reality. Christians retreated from trying to influence the world for truth and righteousness.

William Jennings Bryan died just a few days after the Scopes Trial. If he were alive today, he would certainly be distressed at the inability of individual Christians and the church to articulate and apply a biblical worldview in society. Throughout his public life, Bryan's clarion call was loud and clear: It does not matter if you feel small or insignificant; if you have the truth, you can be confident and courageous. He said, "The humblest citizen of all the land, when clad in the armor of a righteous cause, is stronger than all the hosts of error." We admire Bryan because he passionately delivered his message even when it seemed the whole world was against him.

Once you begin cultivating a passion for *your* message, the delivery skills of visual directness, physical energy, and vocal enthusiasm will help you communicate it powerfully to your audience. When William Jennings Bryan spoke, his audiences *felt* his passion because he expressed it confidently and courageously. You will find this same ability growing in your life. This chapter will boost your chances for success by equipping you with specific strategies for mastering the fundamentals of speech delivery.

As we discussed in Chapter Two, fear is your enemy. It causes doubt. It paralyzes you, preventing your answering questions or responding properly in difficult situations. Passion conquers fear by reinforcing your sense of mission. If you care deeply about your subject and are convinced the audience needs to hear it, you can master fear by telling yourself, "The audience *needs* this information. If they do not hear it from me, they may never hear it."

The key to effective delivery, then, is to focus on passion and mission. Think of it this way: Passion is the banquet you have prepared for the audience, and delivery skills help you arrange the feast to make it inviting. While your enthusiasm makes the message appealing, your delivery skills make it irresistible.

Delivery Skills Make Your Message Irresistible

The skills necessary for speaking in front of a group are quite similar to those needed for one-on-one commu-

> "I have now disposed of all my property to my family. There is one thing more I wish I could give them, and that is the Christian religion."
>
> —Patrick Henry

> "As individuals professing a holy religion, it is our bounden duty to forgive injuries done us as individuals. But when to the character of Christian you add the character of patriot, you are in a different situation.... When you consider injuries done to your country your political duty tells you of vengeance. Forgive as a private man, but never forgive public injuries."
>
> – Patrick Henry
> cited by William Wirt
> Henry in 1891

nication: eye contact, organized ideas, clear examples, a confident manner, good posture, a clear speaking voice, and a sense of caring about the audience. If you can master these skills in front of a group, then translating them into your personal relationships will be much easier. Moreover, you will find yourself becoming aware of good and bad communication around you, and this awareness helps you further improve your communication style.

Some public speaking teachers list dozens of things a speaker should remember about effective delivery. I list only three: visual directness, physical energy, and vocal enthusiasm. I have taught them successfully to thousands of high school students, college students, and adults. They are not difficult to learn, but they take practice to master. The good news is that by working at them, you will notice your skill and confidence growing rapidly. Let's examine each of these delivery skills in turn.

Visual Directness: Connecting With the Audience

Some well meaning speech teachers say, "If it makes you uncomfortable to look audience members in the eye, then look at their foreheads or at the back wall." This advice, however well-intentioned, is wrong. Maintaining direct eye contact with members of your audience communicates authenticity, maintains the audience's attention, and allows you to receive feedback. In short, it is essential.

Researchers tell us that the most effective eye contact takes about *three to seven seconds per audience member*. This is the amount of time it takes to look a member of your audience in the eye, have them become aware of your contact, and respond—either by nodding, smiling, raising or furrowing their eyebrows, yawning, or giving you that "don't look at me" look! A wealth of emotions can be conveyed by the human face. Do not pass up this opportunity to discover what your audience really thinks!

Maintaining eye contact long enough to get a response is called a *visual transaction*. As a speech teacher, I practiced visual transactions with students through a game in which each person gave a mini-speech while seven members of the audience raised their hands. The goal of the speaker was to maintain eye contact with each audience member for a full seven seconds without looking away, at which time the person would put their hand down, and the speaker would establish eye contact with the next person. The goal was to knock all of the hands down.

There was a catch, however. I instructed audience members to keep their hands up until the transaction was complete. In other words, if the speaker looked away after four seconds, the audience member would start counting all over again. Eventually, all the students managed to complete their speeches without significant psychological damage! In the process, they became aware of the significance (and the difficulty) of visual directness.

Visual directness is perhaps the hardest part of delivering a speech. Even practiced speakers must concentrate to be successful. If you make it part of your presentation, you will find yourself focusing more on the audience than on yourself. And you will discover that the audience responds more favorably to your speech.

Remember from the video lesson that you *do* want to look at as many audience members as possible, and you want to maintain contact until you are sure they are listening. You will know you are successful when you can gauge a person's response to your speech by his or her facial expressions. You will be *most* successful if you *avoid* writing a speech word for word, reading your speech, staring over people's heads, or quickly scanning the audience. The goal is to establish a *visual transaction* with as many audience members as possible.

Physical Energy: Bringing the Audience to Life

All speakers have some kind of nervous habit which exhibits itself while they are speaking. One of my teachers in middle school tugged at her ear. Students made a game of counting how many times she fiddled with her ear during each class. This nervous habit diminished the power of her message.

Even Ronald Reagan, great communicator that he was, had nervous habits. Invariably, he began his speeches by dipping his head, grinning sheepishly, and starting his sentences with, "Well…." Comedians imitated him mercilessly, just as they do with political figures today.

The nervousness produced by a public performance is your body's natural response to a feeling of danger. God designed your body to produce extra energy so you can handle threatening situations.

Your goal is not to eliminate nervous energy but to use it to your benefit. That is why physical energy is such an important delivery skill. It enables you to work off excess energy by expressing yourself enthusiastically. The "energy release principle" taught in the video helps you view nervousness as *energy* rather than *fear*. Effective speakers "throw" their energy into the audience by using exaggerated gestures and animated movements.

While using wide gestures may feel awkward to you, it looks perfectly normal to the audience. Stage actors use extremely exaggerated movements, but the audience views it as natural. In fact, actors who do not exaggerate their motions appear stilted and lifeless.

When you give a speech, let your nervous energy express itself as confidence and enthusiasm for your speech topic. It will help you relax, and when the audience sees you are relaxed and enjoying yourself, they will be more likely to enjoy themselves as well.

So let's recap. Employing the energy release principle, be sure to use wide gestures and move around occasionally. Use movement to help you make

> "This is all the inheritance I can give to my dear family. The religion of Christ can give them one which will make them rich indeed."
>
> —Patrick Henry
> In his will

> "We are descended from a people whose government was founded on liberty.... That country is become a great, mighty, and splendid nation; not because their government is strong and energetic, but, sir, because liberty is its direct end and foundation. We drew the spirit of liberty from our British ancestors; by that spirit we have triumphed over every difficulty."
>
> –Patrick Henry
> **Virginia Constitutional Convention June, 1788**

a point. Move away from the podium, stand close to the audience, and lean forward slightly to show that you are involved.

As you practice the energy release principle, you also should become sensitive to habits that the audience would find distracting, such as pacing, rocking back and forth, mechanical movements, or unusual mannerisms. Watching a videotape of your speech will help you become aware of what you need to change.

Now that we have checked out how to channel physical energy through the energy release principle, let's turn our attention to the third vital delivery skill, vocal enthusiasm.

Vocal Enthusiasm: Keeping the Audience Interested

You're tense. You feel trapped. You wonder if it is ever going to end. A nightmare? Nope. Few things are less enjoyable or meaningful than listening to a monotonous speaker. Time drags like a sea turtle in the desert. You wonder, "If *they* can't get excited about this topic, why should *I* care about it?"

Fortunately, enthusiasm is even more contagious than boredom. An enthusiastic voice relieves the tension between you and the audience. It causes a positive audience response and conveys the impression that you really care about your message. Moreover, vocal enthusiasm forces you to be expressive and makes the speech that much more enjoyable for you and the audience.

Vocal enthusiasm is so powerful that I have witnessed speakers giving successful speeches through the power of vocal enthusiasm *alone.* I recall all too well my first keynote address at a major convention. Before I was to speak, the lobbyist for the organization was scheduled to give a 15-minute update on the activity of the state legislature. I have heard many presentations like this, most of them lacking in enthusiasm. I resigned myself to letting this guy put my audience to sleep just before I was to speak.

What happened next was totally unexpected. The lobbyist took the stage and, at the volume of the hot-dog vendor at a baseball game, hit the audience with all he was worth. He inspired such enthusiasm that he received three standing ovations. Unfortunately, by the time I was ready to take the stage, the audience was worn out!

Enthusiasm originates in your voice. A slow, dull, monotone voice destroys enthusiasm. A confident voice with variety and sparkle spreads it. You can convey enthusiasm through every speech you give by: (1) entrusting your message to the audience, (2) practicing vocal variety, and (3) using creative language.

1. Entrust your message to the audience.

Believe in your audience. See them as worthy of your best efforts. Most audiences are on your side, so give them a chance to warm up to you, and you will find them friendly, receptive, and responsive. Your voice is your main tool for inspiring enthusiasm in this way. *Believe* that the audience will learn something from your presentation. Create anticipation by offering a few hints about what they will learn. Use your voice to show that you are excited about your topic and the opportunity to communicate it to them.

I know many speakers who are enthusiastic and hard-hitting. I have watched one particular individual for years. He treats audiences with respect, delighting them with more information than they were expecting. When speaking several times to the same audience, he uses his early talks to build up suspense for later talks. I recall one seminar in which this speaker was to give four lectures in a row, with ten minute breaks in between. The audience pleaded with him to skip the breaks and continue speaking. *He spoke for four hours with no breaks, and the audience still did not want to leave!* He trusted the audience, and they in turn trusted him.

By the way, here is a tip for creating a sense of anticipation that will dramatically increase your effectiveness as a speaker. You can add pizzazz to any speech by persuading your audiences of the *value* your material will bring into their lives. For example:

Many people feel that their lives just don't count. They are discouraged. They feel devoid of meaning and purpose. They lack fulfillment. But when they encounter the truth that I am going to share with you this afternoon, everything begins to change. They develop boldness. Their lives become more meaningful. They become convinced that they can make a difference and that what they do really does matter. Before we get to that great truth, however, we need to identify the source of this sense of discouragement....

A warning is in order here. If you make a promise, you *must* deliver. Your points *must* be meaningful, and they *must* answer the questions you raise. Otherwise, the audience will feel cheated, and when they feel cheated, they'll be angry. And when they get angry, guess who they take it out on? You. That said, a well-planned introduction helps your audience anticipate what you will say. And that gives you confidence, which increases the audience's enthusiasm and so forth.

2. Practice vocal variety.

Vocal variety simply means making your voice interesting. I know of one speaker who likes to start out softly, and continue softly until the audience is absolutely silent. Then he broadens his inflection, maintaining a very relaxed, controlled, yet interesting voice. Each person has a comfort zone. I encourage you to find yours and expand it by telling stories and adding dramatic flourishes. There are three keys to vocal variety:

> "Cultivate your mind by the perusal of those books which instruct while they amuse. Do not devote much of your time to novels.... History, geography, poetry, moral essays, biography, travels, sermons, and other well-written religious productions will not fail to enlarge your understanding, to render you a more agreeable companion, and to exalt your virtue."
>
> —Patrick Henry
> Letter to daughter Annie

> "I have but one lamp by which my feet are guided, and that is the lamp of experience. I know no way of judging of the future but by the past."
>
> —Patrick Henry
> St. Johns Church March 1775

• Pitch—raise and lower the *tone* of your voice.

• Volume—raise and lower the *loudness* of your voice.

• Pace—speed up and slow down the *pace* of your words.

With each of these, *change* is the key. A speaker who is always loud is just as tiresome as a speaker who always speaks too softly. It is helpful to practice your speech aloud to hear how the words sound when spoken. In your notes, underline key points so you will remember to slow down and emphasize them. A good speaker's notes will be full of meaningful underlining, highlighting, bold characters, stars, and cues in the margin.

Here's a quick coaching point as you prepare: if you merely read the speech, you are wasting the audience's time. They could read it themselves much more quickly. The audience is relying on you to highlight what is important and to convince them that what you say is true. Words alone don't do this. Vocal variety *does*.

3. Use creative language.

Another way vocal enthusiasm can bring a speech to life is through the use of creative language. By creative language I mean dialogue, vivid description, character development, and a sense of plot. Here are two examples:

(1) Describing how a close friend met his future bride:

Uncreative:
"Tom asked her to go to the party and she said yes."

Creative:

Shaking and terrified, Tom said, "W-w-would y-you go with me to the annual fireman's ball next weekend?" Her sultry reply excited every fiber of his being. "Yes, I would love to," she replied with a heart-melting smile.

(2) Introducing a long-time friend to a fun audience at a fun occasion:

Uncreative:

"Please welcome our next speaker, your friend and my friend, Joe."

Creative:

"Our next speaker has been my boisterous compatriot for more than five years. He comes to us from the thriving metropolis of Pine Grove, where he is the mayor, sheriff, postmaster, dog catcher, and weed control supervisor. There are many adjectives I could use to describe Joe, but the vast majority of them are not suitable for polite company such as we have this evening. So, we might as well get it over with. Here's my good friend, and your friend too, if you'll claim him, Joe."

As you become a more skillful speaker, try to develop a sense of "plot" in your speech. Draw the audience into the mystery of the moment. Create excitement by using a key person from history to illustrate points in your talk. Radio commentator Paul Harvey has used this method with great effect. He reveals intriguing details about a person's life, but withholds the name until the end to build suspense.

Let's review the key points about vocal enthusiasm. First, remember that enthusiasm is contagious. Convey your excitement for your topic through your voice, and use creative techniques to surprise and delight the audience. Second, be assertive. Speak confidently. Do not let your sentences trail off at the end, or end in a questioning tone as if you are looking to the audience for affirmation.

Avoid a boring monotone voice at all costs. Practice your speech in advance to create vocal variety. Avoid vocal crutches such as, "you know," "um," and "okay." Finally, remember that audience members interpret poor grammar as a lack of intelligence. Find a knowledgeable person to coach you on using words properly.

Delivery Skills Help You in Everyday Life

The same skills which help you deliver a message to an audience can help convey your confidence, caring, and trustworthiness in everyday life. The way you greet others, the way you an-swer the telephone, and the response you give when someone asks, "How are you?" all indicate your excitement about life and about your mission. Look people in the eye, use good posture, and speak confidently. Express interest in others. Discuss your speech ideas and stories with others in conversation. This will help you develop leadership skills and increase your influence in everyday life.

The Most Important Delivery Skill of All

There is one final skill which is so essential to effective speech delivery that I consider it to be the most important delivery skill of all: *observation.* Sharp powers of observation make it easier to gather information, figure out what people are thinking, and relate better to them. The Apostle Paul's speech to the Athenians is a model in this regard. Paul invested time talking with people, observing their customs, and even reading their literature. When it came time to speak to them, he knew exactly how they might be persuaded.

Sharp powers of observation also help you quickly learn which speech techniques are effective and which ones are not. Just *watch* the positive and negative habits of other speakers. If you see something that works, try it out yourself. If you notice a habit that is counterproductive, avoid it.

Finally, sharp powers of observation help you improve your skills. Effective speakers seek feedback from the audi-

"In the management of your domestic concerns let prudence and wise economy prevail. Let neatness, order, and judgement be seen in all your different deportments. Unite liberality with a just frugality; always reserve something for the hand of charity; and never let your door be closed to the voice of suffering humanity."

—Patrick Henry
Letter to daughter Annie

> "I live much retired, amidst a multiplicity of blessings from the Gracious Ruler of all things, to whom I owe unceasing acknowledgments for his unmerited goodness to me; and if I was permitted to add to the catalogue one other blessing, it should be that my countrymen should learn wisdom and virtue, and in this their day to know the things that pertain to their peace."
>
> – Patrick Henry
> To Archibald Blair after Henry's retirement

ence, both during the speech as well as through interviews and questionnaires after it is over. What did they like? What do they wish there was more time for? What did *not* make sense? You can also videotape or audiotape your speeches and review them. Better yet, review them with people who are respectable communicators in their own right. Give people permission to suggest ways you can improve. This will seem a little awkward at first, but in time you will notice your speeches getting better and better, and audiences becoming more and more responsive.

If you can master the three delivery skills, *visual directness, physical energy, and vocal enthusiasm,* you will have won a large part of the battle of becoming a superb communicator. Equipped with the confidence that your strength and ability are from God, you will deliver truth to the heart of any audience and make an enormous difference in the world.

Three Steps to Take Right Now

In the following pages you will find

(1) **Personal Application** worksheet to journal your thoughts about delivery skills;

(2) **Delivery Skill Awareness Worksheet** to catalog feedback about your speech, and

(3) **"Delivery Skills" Speech Project.**

You are nearing the end of the *Secrets of Great Communicators* coaching system! There is only one more step: cultivating opportunities to use speech-giving to influence others. In Chapter Six, you'll discover the secrets of an unforgettable speech!

Personal Application

1. List some of the benefits of visual directness. List some of the problems of not maintaining visual directness.

2. List the three most effective speakers you have observed. What delivery skills have they mastered?

"If you have a good President, senators and represent-atives, there is no danger. But can this be expected from human nature? Without real checks, it will not suffice that some of them are good.... Virtue will slumber: the wicked will be continually watching: consequently you will be undone."

– Patrick Henry
Virginia Constitutional Convention, June 1788

3. What are your greatest struggles with each of the three delivery skills? Decide how you can go about improving in each area.

• Visual directness:

Strategy for improving:

"You are created in the image of Almighty God. God is a communicative God. He made you to communicate, and you can do it because you are made in His image."

– Jeff Myers

• Physical Energy:

Strategy for improving:

• Vocal enthusiasm:

Strategy for improving:

Delivery Skill Awareness Worksheet

Videotape your speech and evaluate it with these questions.

- **Visual Directness:**

  Did you look audience members in the eye? Did you tend to quickly scan the audience, or did you slowly and deliberately look at each person?

  How many times did you look an audience member in the eye until they responded (with a nod, a smile, etc.)?

  What proportion of your speech do you spend looking at your notes (ideal is less than 20%)?

  List two things you can work on to improve your visual directness.

PLANNING TIP

Remembering key points:

1. Keep it simple. Colored pens or highlighters can be distracting.

2. Make it visible. Black ink on yellow legal paper is most visible.

3. Practice your speech to make sure you recall what your notations mean.

4. Put key words in all caps.

5. Underline quotes so they will be easy to find by glancing down.

6. Put stars next to points that deserve greater emphasis.

7. Make margin notes brief to quickly recall what to do.

REMINDER—The Energy Release Principle:

When you channel your nervous energy into expressiveness, you appear confident and relaxed. This, in turn, helps the audience relax and enjoy the experience, which makes them more fun to speak to.

• **Physical Energy:**

List the barriers that came between you and the audience (standing behind the lectern, gripping or playing with the lectern, etc.)

What steps did you take to throw your energy into the audience?

List any mannerisms you used that might be distracting to the audience.

List two things you will do differently next time with your physical energy.

- **Vocal Enthusiasm:**

List what you did to express enthusiasm to the audience. Did your voice convey variety?

List any difficulties you noticed on the tape (saying "um," bad grammar, voice too soft or too loud, etc.)

List two steps you can take to improve vocal variety:

"Delivery Skills" Speech Project

The speech project for this chapter will give you the opportunity to rehearse a *7-10 minute speech* which you already have prepared, in order to focus on and improve your speech delivery skills.

Here are some guidelines to follow as you prepare:

1. **Select an existing speech. For best results, choose a speech that you feel confident giving, one which is interesting to you and to the audience.**

2. **Convert the speech into outline form. Except for the introduction, key points, and transitions, your speech should not be written out word for word. Use the minimum number of words you can while still remembering what to say (see the sample speech which follows).**

3. **Review your outline. Highlight key points, and write brief instructions for yourself which will help you adequately emphasize each point to the audience.**

4. **Practice giving the speech. Record your speech on videotape if possible. If not, create a makeshift lecturn and give the speech as you would in front of an audience. Focus on the delivery skills of physical energy and vocal enthusiasm.**

5. **Review your speech. Using your "Delivery Skills Awareness Worksheet," analyze your speech to determine ways to improve.**

PLANNING TIP

Effective Outlining of a Speech

1. Write out the first 50 words. Memorize this part.

2. Develop the outline based on the attention, need, solution, and action steps.

3. Use key words rather than full sentences where possible. Practice them to be sure you can convey each point clearly.

4, Write out full sentences only for quotations or difficult points that must be conveyed precisely.

Sample Speech Outline with Notations

[The following is an outline of the sample speech from Chapter Four, along with speaker notations]

I. I once heard of a church where members thought it was against God's will to vote. They <u>prayed</u> that the right person would win, but they themselves refused to participate. In one election, there was a choice between two candidates: one was good and moral, the other shifty and unscrupulous. Concerned, 50 members of the church gathered for an all-night prayer vigil, but in the morning, they refused to vote. <u>The good candidate lost by 35 votes.</u> **!!**

    A. Extreme example-extreme problem. Participation going down

> Move to side of podium

    B. Purpose: **(1)** Convince you that not voting = serious, **(2)** challenge to get involved.

II. The problem: <u>when people do not vote, our very system of government is in danger.</u>

    A. Benjamin Franklin—"Mr. Franklin, what sort of government have you given us?" Franklin replied, "A republic, madam, <u>if</u> <u>you</u> <u>can</u> <u>keep</u> <u>it</u>."

    B. Republic—not voting = lost opportunity to express opinions.

    C. <u>People become apathetic, republic perishes.</u>

    D. Youth need to take this citizenship responsibility seriously.

> "Youth have not always been encouraged to be politically involved"

        1. 1971, youth vote for first time: 26th amendment to the Constitution: "The right of citizens of the United States, who are eighteen years of age or older, to vote shall not be denied or abridged by the United States or by any State on account of age."

        2. Voter News Service: 18-32 year-olds vote in lower number than any other generation. 1/3 of eligible voters, less than 25% of the actual voters.

    E. Young voters expressing views by staying away from the polls.

> Downward spiral

    F. <u>Trust in government</u> and <u>interest in civic concerns</u>—all time low.

SPEAKER'S NOTES

1. Because they <u>aren't</u> <u>interested</u>, they <u>don't</u> <u>vote</u>.

2. Because they <u>don't</u> <u>vote</u>, their <u>interests are not represented</u>.

3. Because their <u>interests are not represented</u>, young people have <u>no voice</u>.

4. Because young people have <u>no voice</u>, they <u>lose interest</u> and <u>trust</u>.

G. Former employee of Project Vote Smart: "by refusing to participate in the voting process, we are <u>blindly</u> turning over complete control on these issues to institutions we don't trust to make decisions in our own best interests."

H. Political Communication course example: only two of the students actually voted, most weren't even <u>registered</u> to vote. Yet they had **complained** day after day in class about the lack of Christian influence in government.

Ask for show of hands >

I. Truth time. How many have ever criticized or expressed mistrust of a public official?

1. Vast majority wish things were different. Easy to talk about "other people" but let's make it personal.

"You don't have to raise your hand on this one!

2. How involved are <u>you</u>? How are <u>you</u> exercising your responsibilities as a citizen?

III. Solution is simple: register to vote/participate

A. Easy. Forms (1) driver's license bureau, (2) court house, (3) government office building.

1. Apply on-line, or when getting your driver's license.

Explain this >

2. Watch newspaper when and where to vote. Going to be away? Vote absentee. Order on-line or call voter registration office.

B. College example: decided to take voter registration seriously

1. Internet technology, announcements, a poster campaign, and chapel speeches

2. Almost 100% of the students registered to vote, and actual participation was about 80%, about four times the level of involvement by most people of college age.

C. Imagine the incredible changes that could result if good people would go to the polls.

1. 80 million Christians in America began to exercise their right to vote in large numbers? <u>No election even close.</u>

2. Pro-family, pro-morality candidates elected to the school board, the city council, state legislature, governorship, Congress, and even the presidency.

3. All it takes is <u>one vote</u>…by a <u>concerned citizen</u>…<u>times millions of concerned citizens.</u>

D. You may say, "this all sounds great, but it can't be that easy. It is hard to register to vote." Or, "Christians shouldn't get involved in such a dirty business." Or, you might even be discouraged, saying "My little vote won't make a difference." Let me deal with each of these objections in turn.

1. Difficulty. Not hard. Voter registration forms for everyone in the audience. Fill out, I'll take to the courthouse for you, you will receive registration card in mail.

2. Christians getting involved. <u>Politics gets dirty because good people fail to get involved.</u>

a. Matthew 28:18 Jesus said, "<u>All authority</u> has been given to Me in heaven and on earth." Jesus has authority over all areas of life, including politics.

b. William L. Fisher of the Christian Coalition suggests that Jesus' authority gives us the right to ("ask Christians to do their part to bring Christian values to the shaping of public policy.")

3. <u>Whether one vote makes a difference:</u>

a. One vote gave Thomas Jefferson the presidency over Aaron Burr.

b. In 1868, one vote saved Andrew Johnson's presidency.

c. In 1960, 1 vote per precinct gave JFK the presidency.

d. <u>One vote did make a difference. That vote could be yours.</u>

> < Slow, intense—big vision

> > Upward spiral

> < History shows the remarkable significance of each vote!

121

SPEAKER'S NOTES

e. Dr. Terry Moffitt, a political consultant, says, "If you don't vote, <u>you</u> <u>are</u> <u>irrelevant</u>. <u>You lose your right to complain</u>."

f. It is especially important for good people with solid values to get involved and try to shape the public policy process in a direction that shows our obedience to God.

Get helpers—wait until everyone has theirs to continue >

IV. Conclusion. Hand out the voter registration forms.

A. Already registered? Just write your name, street address and e-mail address, and put "already registered." I'll contact you with info on next election and where you will vote.

B. It will only take 30 seconds—most important 30 seconds you could invest.

C. Abraham Lincoln, Gettysburg Address, he strongly resolved that "government of the people, by the people, and for the people, shall not perish from the earth."

D. Hundreds of thousands of men and women have died to protect your right to vote. <u>Do not let their deaths be in vain.</u>

"Thank you" =>
Collect forms

DISCOVER THE SECRETS OF AN UNFORGETTABLE SPEECH

(21 minutes)

1. Be aware of speech _____.

2. Be good at communication _____ and _____ the speech.

3. Be thinking about speech material _____ the _____.

4. Be _____ to the audience's needs and desires.

5. Be _____ about what is important.

6. Be _____.

7. Be _____ about your subject.

8. Be funny in a _____ way.

9. Be in _____ of the speech situation

CHAPTER SIX

Discover the Secrets of an Unforgettable Speech

KEY QUOTE:

KEY QUOTE:

A speech is really a conversation. Just be yourself. When you relax, the audience relaxes, and they are more likely to hear what you have to say.
—Jeff Myers

Focus on Great Communicators:
Billy Graham

CHAPTER AT A GLANCE

- A diamond in the rough.
- Here I am—send me!
- Becoming a bearer of redemption.
- It's your turn now.
- Six strategies for getting invited to speak.
- Excelling at communication before and after the speech.
- Discover rich lodes of speech material by thinking of speeches all the time.
- How to communicate grace without compromising truth.
- Be yourself, and persuade audiences through authenticity.
- Be convincing by being enthusiastic about your subject.
- Surprise and delight your audience with humor that is naturally you.
- Gain confidence by being prepared and in control of the speech situation.
- What to say when something goes wrong.
- How to handle hecklers.
- Considering the audience's needs.
- Congratulate yourself!

BILLY GRAHAM HAS BEEN CALLED "America's pastor." *Time* magazine recognized him as one of the 100 most influential men of the 20th century. More than 200 million people have made professions of faith through his ministry.

Yet like many other great communicators, Graham had an inauspicious beginning. At age 18, he enrolled in a Bible institute and was encouraged by his teachers to memorize four thirty-minute sermons. When asked to preach, he was so nervous that he blasted out all four of his sermons in 10 minutes!

> "Christians should never fail to sense the operation of an angelic glory. It forever eclipses the world of demonic powers, as the sun does a candle's light."
>
> —Billy Graham

Graham's biographer wrote, "Billy flailed the air with his pipe-stem arms, pounced around the pulpit like a man swatting flies, boomed his raw North Carolina twang to the far pews."

Audiences were so stunned by his rapid fire delivery that they did not know what to make of him. His family was embarrassed and doubted his calling. Yet Graham preached a simple message, one that he continued to preach until well into his 80s: "We are all sinners. Christ died to pay for our sins, and we must accept Him in order to be saved."

The Billy Graham Evangelistic Association is considered a model of integrity and sincerity. Graham has received much criticism by liberals for proclaiming a "simple" gospel and by conservative fundamentalists for associating with Catholics and liberal Protestants. Nevertheless, the self-proclaimed country boy has preached the same simple message all over the world. "When God gets ready to shake America," he once said, "He may not take the Ph.D. and the D.D. God may choose a country boy…and I pray that he would!"

A Diamond in the Rough

In the late 1600s an adventurer named Jean Baptiste Tavernier met with Louis XIV, King of France, to show the treasures he had brought from India. One was a 112 carat, violet-hued diamond. King Louis loved it and purchased it from Tavernier, along with 14 other smaller diamonds.

Through the centuries, this diamond has been cut, reshaped, reset, and resold, and today it is known as the "Hope Diamond." At 45.52 carats, this apparently flawless gem is still believed to be the world's largest deep blue diamond. It is so valuable that on a recent trip to be cleaned and reset, the Hope Diamond was accompanied by a team of 40 S. W. A. T. officers.

Long ago, however, the Hope Diamond was merely a lump of rock buried deep in the earth. Thrust to the surface by a volcanic eruption, it was not until the diamond was cleaned, cut, and polished that its stunning beauty was revealed. With each refinement, it has become even more beautiful and valuable.

Diamonds have no light source of their own; they merely reflect light dramatically because of their complex design. You are the same way—a diamond in the rough. God created you in his image and is cutting, shaping, cleaning, and polishing you to reflect His glory more and more as time goes by. The magnificence of your life testifies to the awesomeness of God's design.

As you have worked through *Secrets of Great Communicators*, you have learned how to cooperate with God's plan by chipping away at fear, organizing your thoughts, and polishing your skills. Each time you communicate effectively, you reflect God's light more brilliantly.

We have now arrived at Chapter Six, and all the pieces are in place for your emergence as a great communicator. What remains is finding opportunities for your continued growth and development as a speaker. In this chapter you will learn:

- How to achieve long-term success as a communicator.

- How to discover rich lodes of speech material.

- How to persuade audiences through your authenticity.

- How to communicate with enthusiasm and humor.

- How to be confidently in control of a speech situation.

In a way, I envy you. I wish someone had shared these points with me when I was beginning as a communicator. I trust God will use these principles in your life to shape you into a world-changing communicator, just as he used them in the life of a terrified prophet long ago.

Here I Am—Send Me!

The vision must have been shocking: "I saw the Lord seated on a high and lofty throne, and His robe filled the temple. Seraphim were standing above Him… And one called to another: 'Holy, holy, holy is the Lord of Hosts; His glory fills the whole earth.'"

At this vision, Isaiah, whose name meant "The Lord Saves" was nearly undone. "Woe is me," he cried, "for I am ruined, because I am a man of unclean lips!"

Yet when the Lord said, "Who should I send? Who will go for Us?" Isaiah replied, "Here I am. Send me" (Isaiah 6, selected verses).

"Here I am. Send me." Now *that* is a statement of faith. No matter how overwhelming the task seemed, Isaiah was willing to act on God's call.

The people of Isaiah's day had forgotten God. They practiced witchcraft, worshipped pagan gods, and were shamelessly evil, decadent, and arrogant. Rather than loving their neighbors, they oppressed them. Rather than seeking justice, they convicted the innocent, and worst of all, they reveled in their corruption.

Isaiah's message was this: Repent or be destroyed. Mind you, this is probably not a message Isaiah *wanted* to deliver. He would probably have preferred to deliver a message of hope, that everything would be just fine.

Becoming a Bearer of Redemption

Though Isaiah's message seemed dark, it actually was in one sense a message of hope. He predicted the fall of Jerusalem to Babylon, yet he also prophesied that a Messiah would come and restore God's people to their former glory:

Prepare the way of the Lord in the wilderness; make a straight highway

> "…you are not alone. All mankind is traveling with you, for all mankind is on this same quest. All humanity is seeking the answer to the confusion, the moral sickness, the spiritual emptiness that oppresses the world. All mankind is crying out for guidance, for comfort, for peace."
>
> —Billy Graham
> *Peace With God: Revised and Expanded* (Carmel, NY: Guideposts, 1984), p. 13

> "Study the Bible constantly. That's where I think I have failed. I don't know the Bible nearly as well as I wish I did, and I wish I spent more time studying it."
>
> —Bill Graham
> AOL Chat
> July 1999

for our God in the desert. Every valley will be lifted up, and every montain and hill will be leveled; the uneven ground will become smooth, and the rough places a plain. And the glory of the Lord will appear, and all humanity will see [it] together, for the mouth of the Lord has spoken (Isaiah 40:3-5).

The people of Isaiah's day had fallen into sin, just as people have in every age. Yet God provided a way out if they would just receive it. In our day, God's message of redemption is the same. Christians are bearers of that redemption, calling society out of its complacency and desperation to hope and comfort. Isaiah gave the message willingly, and that made him a great communicator.

In this segment of *Secrets of Great Communicators* you will discover the secrets of an unforgettable speech. These secrets will reveal how to exercise your growing influence to find and cultivate opportunities to speak. They will empower you to unleash your passion and to influence others.

As you reach the end of this coaching system, God may be preparing you to reach whole nations, or he may be equipping you to reach just a few individuals. The numbers are irrelevant. Your success will lie in how consistently you speak the truth which brings redemption to a world that desperately needs it. Your willingness to say "Here I am—send me" will make all the difference in this generation and for generations to come.

It's Your Turn Now

So. You have a speech, one that you have refined and delivered several times—a speech you are passionate about. Now it is time to create a strategy to use this speech—as well as others you develop through time—to inspire and influence others.

In this chapter, we will explore the secrets of success in public speaking by expanding on the strategies that great communicators use to create opportunity and influence.

Six Strategies for Getting Invited to Speak

Once you finish the *Secrets of Great Communicators*, one of your challenges will be to get invited to give your speech. I have described for you below the steps you need to take to accomplish this.

1. Develop a clever title for your speech.

A clever title gives information about the topic *in terms of* the benefit a person would receive by listening to it. In college I developed a speech for community organizations about what my generation of college students would be like in the workplace. A compelling title for this type of seminar might be: "Workers of the Future: How Generation X can Prosper Your Business in the New Economy."

2. Develop a 4 sentence description of the speech.

One trick I have learned as a speaker is to develop a four-sentence description of my speech. Done well, these four sentences will make people insatiably curious. Here's what you need to do:

1. Give the "background" of the topic–why the speech is necessary.

2. Describe yourself and your qualifications.

3. Briefly outline what you will be talking about.

4. Explain the benefits a person will receive by listening.

Even if you do not feel qualified, you can still excel at this, and I will show you how. Assume, for example, I am still in college giving the "Workers of the Future" speech. Here is what I would say to promote the speech:Generation X: you've heard all the negative clichés. But those who understand and attract Gen-X employees will be poised to prosper in the new millennium. Our speaker, Jeff Myers, is uniquely qualified to talk about this topic: while yet a college student, Jeff has invested three years studying his peers and gaining insight into their values, beliefs and goals. Based on his research, Jeff will share strategies for tapping into Gen-X'er's creative potential and utilizing their talents to reach your highest business goals.

Does it make you curious? A well-written topic description will have people clamoring to hear your speech. If you deliver on your promises, you will be invited to speak again and again.

3. Begin cultivating contacts.

Find people who might be interested in hearing the speech and offer to give it to their group. Do this by seeking the "Solomons" in your life. Author and speaker Gregg Harris notes that when the Queen of Sheba found out King Solomon was the wisest man who had ever lived, she responded by traveling to "test him with difficult questions" (1 Kings 10:1). Your Solomons are the wise people you know who can help you develop your true potential. They include:

Trusted Friends and Relatives. Don't neglect the obvious. Ask family members if they know of people who might want to hear your speech. As a high school student, my brother, Tim, prepared for a speech contest by going to my father's office to give the speech to employees at break time. It was an excellent way to gain experience before approaching a large audience, and it allowed him to adjust his speech and correct some bad habits before the day of the contest.

Spiritual Advisors. Show your speech topic and description to your pastor. Often pastors will allow you to give a speech to a Sunday School class or in some other church setting. This offers

> "Having been reared on a farm in North Carolina, I know that the time for harvest is critical and may not last long. That is true for the Lord's harvest as well. I firmly believe that this is harvest time for the souls of men and women. We, the church, had better take advantage of it while we can—with everything we have!"
>
> —Billy Graham

> "The happiness which brings enduring worth to life is not the superficial happiness that is dependent on circumstances. It is the happiness and contentment that fills the soul even in the midst of the most distressing circumstances and the most bitter environment. It is the kind of happiness that grins when things go wrong and smiles through the tears."
>
> – Billy Graham

outstanding experience, and because the audience is likely to be friendly, it will give your confidence a much-needed boost. In addition, if your pastor likes your speech, he may be willing to call other pastors to see if they know of speech opportunities. Since many ministers are community leaders, they may know people in community organizations and businesses who would be interested in your presentation as well.

Mentors and coaches. If you want to know how to play a sport, you find a good coach. If you want to explore an occupation or find out how to succeed, you should do the same thing. I actually had a "business coach" who helped me build a Web site, improve my speaking, and develop products. Find the coaches and teachers in your community who have made a difference. Tell them you have admired the way they have prospered in their careers and made a difference in the lives of others. Ask if you can take them to lunch for an hour to ask questions and seek advice. Toward the end of the lunch, show them your topic and description, asking for feedback on finding opportunities to deliver it.

Community leaders. When I delivered "Workers of the Future" in college, I sent a letter of introduction, along with a description of my speech, to all of the community organizations in our town (Rotary, Optimist Clubs, Sertoma, Lions Clubs, Kiwanis, etc.). I wrote to more than 100 organiza-

tions, and followed up the letter with a telephone call. I received more than 30 invitations as a result. At the bottom of my letter, I wrote "P.S.: I know that you occasionally have a speaker cancel. I am available to speak on very short notice. Please give me a call should the need arise." As it turns out, my first several invitations came as a result of another speaker canceling!

4. Ask for recommendations.

If your speech goes well, ask your host for a letter of recommendation to provide other potential hosts. After you collect a few recommendations, compile several sentences from each onto a separate page which you can then forward to your potential hosts. Recommendations are critically important. They show that reasonable people have heard and enjoyed your speech. This takes the suspense out of having you as a speaker (which is a good thing!).

5. Start a database.

Using a contact database such as Microsoft Access™, ACT!™ or Gold-Mine™, keep records of all the people you contact. Set reminders for yourself to follow up your letters with telephone calls. If your records are in the computer, it is a lot easier to use e-mail to communicate with those on your list. This will also simplify contacting people when you develop a new speech.

6. Handle the financial issue properly.

Your first speech opportunities are a chance to develop your skills. Your host may graciously pay for your meal and give you a small gift, such as a pen and pencil set, a plaque, or a gift certificate. Occasionally there may be a small honorarium as well.

As your reputation grows, your speaking may become an income-earning opportunity. If this interests you, pick up a copy of a book like *Speak and Grow Rich* by Dottie and Lilly Walters. The title sounds crass, but the information is valuable and is presented with integrity.

In considering how to make money from speeches, you'll need to think through many issues such as what to charge, how to develop products to go along with your speech, and how to meet the expectations of your host. Start by tape-recording your speech and having copies available for a small fee. With time and practice, you may earn money for speaking! I can personally attest that this is a fun, interesting way to make a living.

Excelling at Communication Before and After the Speech

Securing a speaking engagement is the first step in a long process of expanding your speaking potential. Remember the story in the video lesson about my speaking to a motorcycle club? As

it turns out, the club members were friendly, involved citizens who sincerely wanted to make a difference in the community. Having been caught off-guard that one time, I determined to invest time in analyzing the audience and working hard to fit my speech to the situation. The audience analysis/relationship-building process begins the moment someone requests information about your speech, and it keeps on as long as you continue making speeches. The four practices described below are guides to achieving long-term success.

1. Conduct a *pre*-speech interview.

Once you agree to speak, set up a time to meet with your host in person or by telephone to ask questions about the audience and the speech situation. Use the audience analysis worksheet provided in Chapter Four as a guideline. You do not need to ask *all* of the questions, but make it your goal to understand the audience as well as possible before the big day arrives.

2. Conduct a *post*-speech interview.

When your speech is over, ask your host for feedback. Was it an appropriate length? Was the topic of interest? What did group members say about it? If they liked it, politely request a letter of recommendation to show to others.

> "Courage is contagious. When a brave man takes a stand, the spines of others are often stiffened."
>
> —Billy Graham
> *Readers Digest*
> July, 1964

3. Express your gratitude.

As a new speaker, I mistakenly believed that once the speech was over, the relationship with the host was over as well. Sure, I always sent a thank-you note, but I soon lost contact with those who had so graciously invited me to speak. Now, in addition to sending a thank-you note, I often send a small gift (such as a nice pen with my logo engraved on it) and/or a copy of a book I have written (if you haven't written any books yet, send one by someone else you think they might enjoy). Every once in a while I get extra audio copies made of a speech and send them, along with a note of encouragement, to my hosts. I also keep my eye out for newspaper articles, Web sites, or other information my host might find interesting. In return, I ask for recommendations and names of people who might want to hear my speech.

4. Stay in touch.

In addition to the above efforts, I also send out a weekly e-mail newsletter to those who have heard me speak. This contact has actually become a large part of my business, and it leads to far more speech opportunities than I could ever actually accept. Employ these four steps as consistently as you can. As you do, the demand for your speeches will grow…and grow…and grow.

Discover Rich Lodes of Speech Material by Thinking About Speeches All the Time

Great communicators are constantly aware of their surroundings—that is, they cultivate a heightened sense of what is going on around them and what it means. This awareness deepens the meaning of everyday occurrences. It allows them to use their physical eyesight to gain spiritual insight. They understand things, events, and people in new ways.

Observation is the one skill that makes writers brilliant, speakers witty, and counselors adept at assessing the needs of clients. Do you want to be a successful communicator? Learn to observe and interpret what you see. Those who can cleverly discern the meaning of events may become highly trusted speakers.

Driving from my home to the college where I teach, for example, I pass by a funeral home. Each day I notice posted on the display a name, and sometimes several names, of people whose funerals are being held that day. I wonder, "How old were they? What was their life like? What did they do that had lasting value?" As I wonder about these questions, I tell myself, "You know, Jeff, someday your name is going to be up on a board like that. You cannot control how or when, but you *can* live each day to its fullest until your time comes." It is good motivation, and I have shared it with many audiences to great effect. It is good, the Bible says in Psalm 90:12, "to number our days carefully so that we may develop wisdom in our hearts."

My four favorite ways to look for speech material are described below.

1. Browse through books and magazines.

All good speakers do a lot of research, but much of it is "brainstorming research." I own several thousand books on hundreds of different topics, and they are all excellent sources of information. I often schedule time just to wander around libraries, browsing through books and magazines. I do the same thing in bookstores (especially used bookstores) and newsstands. I pick up a tremendous amount of information about what is going on in the world. I also come across sources of information that I might not ordinarily access. In high school, when I had little money, I went to the offices of medical doctors and lawyers asking for the old magazines from their waiting rooms. I invested nothing but time, but I was regularly able to scour dozens of publications for interesting speech material.

2. Have a paper and pen with you at all times.

Everyday experiences abound with speech examples. Write down your thoughts about events, something that caught your attention (such as a bumper sticker or billboard), conversations with people (even ones you overhear), things that really excite or irritate you, Bible verses from your daily study, or anything else that comes to mind. I carry a notebook with me at all times so I can take notes on lectures, speeches, and sermons. I also listen to talk radio and audiotapes or CDs. Sometimes I turn off the radio and just observe what is going on around me, writing down ideas as they occur.

3. Take advantage of creative moments.

Because we live in such a fast-paced world, it is hard to find time simply to sit and think. Personally, I know the times of day I am most likely to be creative, and so I try to invest that time wisely. Whenever I am writing a new speech, I set aside large blocks of time for thinking, writing, and creating. Take advantage of the times when you feel most creative, and your speeches will improve dramatically.

4. Contemplate your own mission.

Often your best speech ideas will come from the unique experiences and opportunities God gives you. Here is an easy three-step process to reflect on your own mission in life:

(1) Look back. Where did you come from? What experiences have shaped you into what you are today? Who has influenced you positively? What

> "We have resorted to every means to win back the position that Adam lost. We have tried through education, through philosophy, through religion, through governments to throw off our yoke of depravity and sin. All our knowledge, all our inventions, all our developments and ambitious plans move us ahead only a very little before we drop back again to the point from which we started. For we are still making the same mistake that Adam made—we are still trying to be king in our own right, and with our own power, instead of obeying God's laws."
>
> —Billy Graham
> *Peace With God, p.47*

> "The victory is yours. Claim it! It is your birthright. Browning said, 'The best is yet to be.' This doesn't mean the Christian can never suffer defeat or experience low periods in life. But it does mean that the Savior goes with you no matter the problem. The peace comes in the midst of problems and in spite of them."
>
> —Billy Graham
> *Peace With God*, p. 166

mistakes have you made that you want to be sure not to repeat? I find that by looking back over my life, I can discern how God brought me through (or allowed me to go through) shaping experiences. God wants me to learn from those experiences, to be humbly grateful for the good things, and to trust Him for guidance in bad times.

(2) Look around. As Henry Blackaby says in *Experiencing God*, "Find out where God is at work, and go there." What are some needs that you observe —in your family, work, school, church, or community? Where can you contribute? Ask God to bring these needs to your attention. Make a list, pray about it, seek wise counsel, and act on what you know.

(3) Look ahead. Time and money aside, what would you rather be doing? If you had one chance to make a difference, what would you do? Spend some time studying the culture. Read about trends in society to see what kinds of opportunities and challenges lie ahead. What could you do to meet them?

These resources for speech ideas will keep your "idea tank" full, giving you a wealth of relevant examples, statistics, and stories for every public-speaking occasion.

How to Communicate Grace Without Compromising Truth

Throughout this coaching system, you have learned that the most important factor in great communication is a passionate concern for your topic. This passion leads to a dilemma, however. How can you passionately communicate the importance of your topic without alienating the audience?

Great communicators learn to balance their passion for a subject with an awareness of how the audience might feel about it. They learn to communicate their topic forthrightly, but in a way that does not demean the audience or cause them to become defensive.

To master this balance we can learn much from one of the great communicators featured in this series, Queen Esther. Scripture explains that once Esther learned of the impending slaughter of her people, she chose to communicate that vital message in a way that emphasized her concern but did not alienate the king, the one to whom she was delivering the message. Here is what Esther did:

1. Esther was responsible.

By the time the crisis arose, Esther had found favor among those in the king's court. She was gracious, likeable, and responsive to the needs of others.

2. Esther was respectful.

Esther did not force herself into the situation. Rather, she designed a clever plan to invite King Xerxes to dinner. During this time she secured his good will and observed what was important to him. She *gave* before she *got*.

3. Esther represented the king's interests.

Rather than focus on her own needs, Esther appealed to the king based on what was important to him, alerting him to the disloyalty of Haman that threatened his rule.

4. Esther regarded truth more highly than persuasion.

By responding, "If I perish, I perish," Esther demonstrated that *obedience* was more important than *success*.

5. Esther was restrained.

Esther did not engage in a hard sell. Since her cause was just, and she was representing it truthfully, she did not need to engage in manipulation. She merely presented the king with information, which appealed to his own interests, and he was persuaded.

These five points are a model of communicating truth in love. Notice that Esther persuaded gently, even though her topic was gravely urgent. She did not try to convince the king of something that was not in his best interests. She was authentic because her cause was just. Her information was true and aboveboard. She was resourceful in meeting the real needs of the king. Her example shows us how to live rightly, wherever we find ourselves in a pagan culture.

Be Yourself and Persuade Audiences Through Authenticity

At one time or another, all great communicators feel uncertainty. They wonder, "What if the audience doesn't like me? What if they reject my message?" When you feel this way, as you undoubtedly will, keep your focus on communicating a positive first impression in an authentic, meaningful fashion. Do not try to become someone else in order to influence the audience. Rather, work to present *yourself* in a positive light.

All of his life Abraham Lincoln struggled with acceptance. As a man of 23, he said, "Every man is said to have his peculiar ambition....I have no other so great as that of being truly esteemed of my fellow men, by rendering myself worthy of their esteem."

What Lincoln discovered is true for you today: Esteem is achieved by painting the canvas of your life in the rich colors of honesty, humility, and caring, and with the bold brush strokes of integrity. This begins the first time you meet someone. Perhaps the simple acronym "F. I. R. S. T." will help you remember how to make a positive im-

> "If we had more hell in the pulpit, we would have less hell in the pew."
>
> —Billy Graham

> "One race in life is greater than any other race. The Apostle Paul must have been interested in races and games because he talked about fighting the good fight and about finishing the course....In ancient Greece winners became heroes. The greatest honor was to be a victor and to receive the reward of an olive branch. But the most important game or race of all is the battle for the souls of people. And that's the race that we all are in right now."
>
> —Billy Graham

pression in a way that reflects integrity of heart.

F = Focus on the audience.

Manipulative communicators ask, "What can this audience do for me?" Great communicators ask instead, "What can *I* do for this audience?" If you maintain a genuine interest in others, you will appear confidently humble rather than overbearing or arrogant.

I = Inquire about their interests.

Find out what the audience cares about. Use your audience analysis worksheet from *Chapter Four* to guide you in discovering their motives and interests. Remember that every person in the audience has hopes and fears, desires and goals. Tie your message to their concerns, and your power as a speaker will grow exponentially.

R = Remember that each person in the audience is made in God's image.

Regardless of your impression of them, other people are created in God's image and are dearly loved by the Creator. Care about them as individuals. Make eye contact with each one. Encompass them with your sense of caring.

S = Smile!

A smile brightens your whole countenance and warms the hearts of others. Fear leads to grim facial expressions which make the audience nervous. Even if your topic is heavy and serious, be warm and friendly.

T = Tell about yourself.

Talk about what interests you, but relate it to their interests. Encourage the audience with your words, empowering them to act.

Be Convincing by Being Enthusiastic About Your Subject

Note well the power of enthusiasm! It is highly contagious. It can be spread with a simple smile, a twinkle in the eye, a quick word of encouragement. People can get it just by *watching* you. Enthusiasm upsets slothfulness, raises one's intellectual temperature, and inspires visions of grandeur. It destroys apathy. It causes self-confidence to ooze out of every pore. The ancient Greeks called it *pathos*—a passion for one's interests that comes across to the audience as power, sincerity and inspiration.

Great communicators express enthusiasm for their audiences by creating value for the people who attend their speeches. Remember: Focusing on how the audience benefits adds power and pizzazz to your speech. Tell your personal story about how this information influenced your life. Highlight the reasons they should care.

Surprise and Delight Your Audience With Humor That Is Naturally You

Using humor appropriately can significantly raise your image as a speaker. Lillian Brown in *Your Public Best* says, "Humor releases your audience and creates a bonding of openness and trust between you and your listeners." Yet few subjects cause as much tension in the minds and hearts of speakers as how to use humor appropriately. What happens if no one gets your joke? What if they don't laugh at the things you find funny?

Fortunately, there are some simple principles that will help you spice your presentation with humor. In *How to Hold Your Audience With Humor*, Gene Perret, a writer for comedian Bob Hope, suggests five strategies for using humor.

1. Test it.

Before you tell a joke to an audience, use it in conversations. Phrase it in different ways to see which gets the biggest reaction. In preparing a talk for parents on how to build communication skills in their children, I wanted to tell a funny story about my daughter, Emma, then age two. Emma had noticed two families (in addition to our own) in which the older children were boys and the younger children were girls. As she reasoned through this, she became convinced in her two-year-old mind that when she got older, she would *become* a boy. One day when I went into Emma's bedroom, Emma asked, "I'm a girl, right?"

I replied, "That's right, Emma."

Emma pressed further: "I'm not a boy, right?"

"That's right, Emma," I said, as I turned to go.

"Well, not yet!" said Emma brightly.

It stopped me in my tracks! It was a very funny thought, Emma believing she would become a boy when she got older. It showed how even little children observe and draw conclusions about the world, often with very charming results.

I wanted to use this story in a speech but found it difficult to communicate how funny it really was. So, I told the story several times to friends, observing how my telling of it brought out the humor in the situation. After getting the wording right, I used the example with an audience. It brought the house down! Practice makes perfect.

2. Be authentic.

Each speaker prefers different kinds of humor. Some like to read top ten lists (a.k.a., talk show host David Letterman); others tell one-liners; others use stories. But sometimes humor is situational and not "jokey" at all. Be very careful about using other people's jokes as your own. Just because it is funny when someone else tells it does not mean it will be funny when you tell it.

Personally, I have found that my best jokes are when I make light of myself.

> "If it is true that 'for every illness there is a cure,' then we must make haste to find it. The sand in civilization's hourglass is rapidly falling away, and if there is a path that leads to the light, if there is a way back to spiritual health, we must not lose an hour!"
>
> —Billy Graham
> *Peace With God*, p. 16

> "Suppose someone should offer me a hamburger after I had eaten a T-bone steak. I would say, 'No, thank you, I am already satisfied.' Young Christian, that is the secret. You are so filled with the things of Christ, so enamored of the things of God, that you do not have time or taste for sinful pleasures of this world."
>
> —Billy Graham
> *Peace With God*, p.159

For instance, I was very insecure, skinny, and awkward as a child. My signature story is about a time when my Christian faith was being challenged in a college class, and I nearly failed to speak up because of insecurity about my body image. To show you how this works, I'll relate how I tell the story:

Growing up, I was always the skinniest kid in my entire class. Skinny arms. Skinny legs. Skinny neck. Of course, that was the 1970s, so I had *big hair*. You can imagine what *that* looked like (this usually gets a pretty good laugh). In fact, when I saw the movie, E.T., I thought, "Wow, I think I was the *model* for that character" (this usually gets a small laugh). So there I was, wanting to stand up for my faith in a college class, with a hostile professor. But I didn't want to do it. I thought, "I'm Jeff Myers, six-feet one inch, only one hundred and forty pounds (long pause). . . No one will even *see* me if I stand up!" (Another big laugh).

People find this story funny because they can relate. Everyone has underlying feelings of insecurity. Laughing at myself breaks the tension and allows the audience to laugh with me (and at themselves). Ultimately, it empowers them to be bold in spite of their own fear.

3. Be consistent.

As you find out what works, repeat the phrasing and timing exactly with each telling. As you rehearse a story, you will find that the phrasing, your vocal variety, the timing, and your facial expressions all affect how funny it is. Once you learn what gets the biggest reaction, tell it *exactly the same way every time*.

4. Don't strain for laughs.

Humor is not an end in itself. It is only useful to refresh your audience and help them remember your message. If you cannot use humor to do that, it is better not to use it at all. If you see that you are losing your audience, it is okay to tell a joke to regain their attention. But be sure the joke is somehow related to the point of your speech. Audiences quickly tire of speakers who allow humor to obstruct their message.

I have had the opportunity to observe hundreds of speakers. Some were absolutely hilarious. Many times after hearing a speech, however, I have thought, "That was very funny, but what exactly was the point?" I firmly believe that if you have to choose between being funny and making your message stick, choose to make your message stick.

If you do not feel confident in your natural humor, pick up some joke books and find stories, quotes, and one-liners that apply to your topic. If you go this route, be mindful of the fact that just because a joke is in a book does not mean it is funny. Test a joke out on your friends before you use it in front of an audience. Moreover, writers of joke books frequently are not very discerning. Many jokes are off-color or demeaning, and such material will quickly destroy your speech. If you have any doubt about a joke's appropriateness, leave it out.

5. Personalize your jokes.

Gene Perret offers one helpful coaching tip that can make a generic joke funnier. He suggests you lure the audience into the joke by setting it up as if it happened to *you*. When you give the punch line, they'll realize they've been had.

Humor can be a great tool, even with a serious topic. Use it wisely, practice it, and with time you will become more naturally funny. You may never be a comedian, but that is not your goal anyway.

Gain Confidence by Being Prepared and in Control of the Speech Situation

As a speaker it is your responsibility to do everything you can to make sure your speech goes smoothly and without disruptions. Where possible, at least an hour in advance, check out the room where you will give your speech. Practice your route to the podium. Test the microphone. Adjust it to your height, and make certain people in the back of the room can hear you without straining. Move things around so you are comfortable. Set up any equipment well in advance and test it. Ask for help if need be, so that you can concentrate on the speech.

When I visit a room where I will be speaking, I take all these steps and a few more. I make sure the chairs are arranged properly. I want people to be fairly close to the podium, so there is not a large open space between me and the audience. If people are sitting at tables, I ask that the tables be tightly grouped rather than spread out to fill the room. I ask for a lapel microphone if possible so I can move around the room and release nervous energy.

When you take these steps, most speeches will proceed according to plan. Audiences will almost always be polite (as long as your speech is not long-winded), and you will be able to give your speech with grace. But every once in a while something happens that you cannot control—a loud noise, a disruptive audience member, or equipment that malfunctions. Since these situations are rare, we will not invest much time talking about what to do. But since disruptions *do* occur, you will feel more comfortable if you have an idea of how to regain control of a faltering speech situation.

Regaining control *is* the key. The question is not whether you lose the audience's attention, but how long it takes to get it back.

> "This generation has been taught that everything is relative. They aren't taught that there are absolutes, such as the Ten Commandments or the person of Christ. Many people are disillusioned with life because they don't have solid, basic truth in their lives. We can tell them about the absolute truth of Jesus Christ, who said, 'I am the way and the truth and the life' (John 14:6)."
>
> – Billy Graham

> "Being a Christian is more than just an instantaneous conversion—it is a daily process whereby you grow to be more and more like Christ."
>
> —Billy Graham

Some time ago, the man who used to be president of the college where I teach, Dr. Bill Brown, was giving a stirring talk in the final chapel of the year. As he spoke, a bat got into the auditorium and began flying around. The audience came apart. It appeared to me that the situation was hopeless—there is *no way* the audience would listen with a bat flying around the room.

As calmly as if he were expecting it, however, Dr. Brown took the PowerPoint™ remote control and began pretending that he was flying the bat like a remote-controlled airplane. People laughed. They watched. Dr. Brown hammed it up, gritting his teeth and swerving around as if he were actually in control of the bat. Eventually the bat flew out of the auditorium. Dr. Brown set down the remote control and with a completely straight face, continued his speech as if nothing had happened. It was hysterically funny, and it worked. He maintained control of the speech situation by *acting* as if he were in control.

What to Say When Something Goes Wrong

I feel more comfortable if I have thought in advance of what to say if something goes wrong. Here is a sampling of possibilities:

• When the microphone squeals: "I guess I should have stayed away from the onions in that salad." (Corny,

but it works with adult audiences. *Do not* use it with teens).

• Microphone crackles as I adjust it to my height: "You may think I'm a public speaker, but in my spare time I practice chiropractic."

• Someone in the adjoining kitchen drops a dish: "Well, there goes my chance for that second helping of dessert!"

• People in the adjoining room laugh or applaud at part of their own event (look toward that room and say, like Elvis): "Thank you. Thank you very much."

• I trip on the platform: "Now you can see why the Olympic team was less than enthusiastic about my application."

• The lights flicker: "Well (host's name), I guess that will be the last time you forget to pay the electric bill!"

• Someone slams a door loudly, making people jump: "Aw, don't go away mad!"

How to Handle Hecklers

We talked briefly in the video lesson about hecklers. We're not talking here about folks who lean over and talks to their neighbor during your speech, or the occasional good-natured comment from an audience member. A heckler a person whose *purpose* is to disrupt your speech, either to call attention to him- or herself or to prevent you from delivering your message. There is very little chance you will have to worry about such individuals. Even with the many speeches I have delivered—a number on controversial topics—I have never faced a genuine heckler in my audience. I have faced hostile audiences, to be sure, but nothing that got out of control. Still, it is best to be prepared. Should you face a heckler, here is a three-step process to be both firm and gracious.

Step One: Acknowledge and defer.

Acknowledge the heckler, and say, "You may have a very valid point. I would appreciate your courtesy in allowing me to finish my message first." They may agree, in which case you should ask to speak to them privately. If you are an accomplished debater, you may wish to ask them to make their remarks publicly so that you may refute them. Otherwise, do what you can to minimize the interruption.

Step Two: Acknowledge and warn.

Acknowledge the heckler, and say, "I will be happy to visit with you personally at the end of the meeting, but I must ask you to stop interrupting my presentation. I would extend the same courtesy if you were in my place, and

the audience and I would appreciate your extending it to me." This may gain the audience's sympathy and make any further interruptions seem unbearably rude.

Step Three: Acknowledge and recess.

Acknowledge the heckler and say, "I am displeased that you have chosen to interrupt my speech. All right. Let's take a five minute break. Everyone, please stand up and stretch and greet those around you. (To the heckler) Sir (or ma'am), the organizers would like to have a word with you." Then, ask the organizers to immediately escort the individual out of the auditorium.

Considering the Audience's Needs.

Throughout this system, I have coached you to put yourself in the audience's shoes, appealing to their motivations and entering their world. Do the same thing in the immediate speech situation to ensure audience members' personal comfort. If the room is too warm or too cool, acknowledge that fact and ask if something can be done. If the audience has been seated for a long time (an hour, usually, is about all a person can take at one sitting), take a few seconds of your speech to allow them to stand and stretch. Stay in control of the situation by asking them to greet those around

"Sometimes I wonder who is going to win the battle first, the barbarians beating at our gates from without, or the termites of immorality from within."

—Billy Graham
Letter to Dwight Eisenhower

them. This will provide a natural ending point to the break.

One time, I heard a former college president speak at a banquet for school administrators. There had been several speeches, as well as entertainment, before his scheduled presentation. By the time he arrived on the podium, audience members had been seated for an hour and a half. Being a seasoned speaker, his first act was to call for a five minute stretch break. Fully *half* the audience bolted for the restrooms! I'm sure that if there had been no break they would have sat politely. But in their discomfort they would have tuned out his speech entirely. Giving the audience a chance to stand up and stretch, and go to the restroom if necessary, refreshed them and made listening easier.

Congratulate Yourself!

Congratulations! Upon completing this coaching system, you are prepared to give a great speech. You also know how to find an audience, and you know what to do when you find one! Although you may still feel jittery, let me assure you that you now have more information and ability than 95% of the population. Just like the great communicators featured in this series, you have extraordinary gifts and opportunities.

Use your newfound public speaking skills however you can. Excel at business presentations. Become a community leader. Teach and encourage people. But whatever you do, remember that your ultimate success will be in proportion to your willingness to die to your fear and live for God.

I experience fear daily. I am tempted to lose heart. When I feel this way, I take courage from a man who lived and died nearly two thousand years ago. His name was Telemachus, and he was a simple monk, a man dedicated to a holy life of prayer and self-denial. Arriving in Rome just after a military victory, Telemachus heard shouts and cheers from within the Coliseum. He joined the crowd and was horrified by what he saw: Romans celebrating their victory by watching gladiators stab and club each other to death.

Telemachus leapt into the arena and said: "Do not requite God's mercy in turning away the swords of your enemies by murdering each other!" The bloodthirsty audience shouted, "Down with him!" The enraged gladiators fell upon Telemachus and killed him. As they backed away, the crowd stared in stunned silence at the body of a man who, in simple-hearted zeal, had challenged the hideous customs of Rome and had paid with his life.

Yet Telemachus had not died in vain. In shame, the Romans left the Coliseum. John Foxe, in *Foxe's Book of Martyrs* claims that Telemachus' death ended the gladiator fights once and for all. Telemachus believed his message so strongly that he was willing to die for it. Yet in his willingness to die, he had experienced life to its fullest and given life to others.

Take courage from Telemachus' example. Your life may never be required of you, but as you die to yourself, you will find strength to truly live, and in living, the strength to speak the truth in love. Let the inspiration of Telemachus drive you on. Be fearless in the face of the world, and you will change the world.

PLANNING TIPS

(1) Organizations that frequently are looking for speakers include churches, social clubs, political organizations, businesses, schools (including colleges), and Bible study groups.

(2) The central "message" you communicate to an audience is usually not the main point of the speech. Rather, it is the impression people come away with about you and about themselves.

Personal Application

Take a few minutes, and jot down responses to these exercises. They will help set your mind toward the task that lies ahead—cultivating and harvesting your speaking potential.

- **List ten individuals or organizations you could approach about giving a speech.**

> "What is ultimately important in life? It is not so much that you become a great communicator or an influential person. The most important thing in life is that you are conformed to the image of Christ."
>
> —Jeff Myers

- **Write down three "life messages" that you want to come through in every speech you give, regardless of topic (for example: "I want to communicate to every audience that they have the power to change their lives in order to gain a higher level of meaning and satisfaction in life").**

Observation Journal

Look around you right now. Brainstorm to come up with three people, objects, or situations that could be used as speech illustrations based on what you see (or read in a book or magazine). They do not have to be good illustrations necessarily—the point is to become accustomed to looking for them. As you develop the habit of observing the world around you, keep a journal of what you see and what it means. Not only will this enhance your understanding of your audience, it will also provide you a lifelong supply of fascinating illustrations.

PLANNING TIP

Use people, objects, and everyday situations as illustrations.

People—Focus on people's attitudes, how they relate, what they are watching, listening to, thinking about, wearing, and spending time on.

Objects—Look at advertisements, paintings, television programs, movies, music, pictures, bumper stickers, or posters. What do they assume about their audience?

Situations—What events have taken place in your life, from which you have learned significant lessons? What is going on culturally, and what does it mean?

Speech Outlines
for Every Occasion

KEY QUOTE:

A speech is really a conversation. Just be yourself.
When you relax, the audience relaxes, and they are more likely to
hear what you have to say.
—Jeff Myers

So...YOU'VE BEEN ASKED TO give the company report. Or speak at a commencement. Or give the eulogy at a funeral. Or introduce a well-known speaker. Even if you have never faced these situations before, you can plan an excellent presentation—that is, if you have the right tools. This appendix contains what you need to help an audience understand your point and participate in the occasion more fully. I predict that, in the long run, you will come to rely on this resource more than just about anything else in this coaching system.

Years ago, Ralph Borden Culp in his book *Basic Types of Speech* (Wm. C. Brown Company Publishers, 1968), offered outlines and strategies for succeeding in the 15 most common speech situations. We have reproduced here, by permission, a list of the terms Dr. Culp commonly uses, as well as the basic outlines he provides for each type of speech. Some of these outlines differ slightly from those presented elsewhere in *Secrets of Great Communicators*, but these differences are minor and will not affect the effectiveness of your speech. Take a few moments to look over these definitions, and then explore the treasure trove Dr. Culp provides.

Definitions of Key Terms

Attention Step

The speaker gains the audience's attention.

Orientation Step

The speaker focuses attention on himself by briefly introducing the subject, history and background, how the subject is relevant to the audience, why the speaker has a right to speak, the purpose of the speech, the main idea of the speech, and how the subject is to be approached.

Identification Step

The speaker produces ideas, images and evidence with which the audience will identify in a favorable way.

Need Step

The speaker attempts to arouse audience needs and motivations, focusing them on the main idea, and creates "cognitive dissonance," the feeling that there is a gap between what is and what ought to be.

Exposition Step

The speaker delves into the topic using a well-organized format which gives the main points, a topic sentence for each, sub-points, supporting evidence, and transitions between topics.

Argumentation Step

The same as the exposition step except that the speaker gives reasons, based on the evidence, for accepting his main idea.

Satisfaction Step

The speaker offers a means of resolving the dissonance created in the need step.

Summation Step

The speaker restates the main points.

Peroration Step

The speaker restates the main idea and if it is a persuasive speech, appeals for action.

Rationalization Step

The speaker gives the audience reasons to act as he is suggesting and works to overcome objections.

Action Step

The speaker actually gives the audience something to do.

Speech Outlines

Speech to Investigate an Issue

This speech format is used to inquire into a situation by: (1) raising pertinent questions, (2) giving the answers which you think are appropriate, and (3) starting a discussion.

I. Attention Step.

II. Orientation Step.

    A. The Problem Area. Describe the area of trouble.

    B. Possible Questions for Discussion. Determine the questions that seem germane and categorize them by type.

    C. The Question for Discussion. Select the one question which, if answered, will solve the problem being studied.

III. Exposition Step.

    A. The Issues in the Question. Discuss all possible problems relevant to the main question.

    B. The Criteria-Answers to Issues. Use the answers to key questions as the criteria by which the final answers will be judged.

    C. The Answer to the Main Question. Measure possible answers against the criteria. The answer should evolve from the inquiry.

IV. Summation Step (Testing the Answer—re-examine the relevant issues and open for discussion).

V. Peroration Step (Set the stage and parameters for the discussion).

Speech to Present a Problem

The purpose of this speech is to bring to the attention of the audience a need or problem.

I. Attention Step.

II. Orientation Step.

III. Need Step (Develop in detail).

    A. Undesirable Effects.
    B. Extensiveness.
    C. Personal Experience.

IV. Summation Step.

V. Peroration Step.

Speech to Present a Solution

This speech is useful when the audience is familiar with the problem but needs to consider supporting a specific proposal.

I. Attention Step.

II. Orientation Step.

A. Review the Problem.
B. Review the Need.

III. Argumentation Step.

A. Statement of the solution or plan.
B. Evidence to support the solution or plan.

IV. Satisfaction or Rationalization Step.

V. Summation Step.

VI. Peroration Step.

Speech to Create Agreement or Action

This format is used when the audience is well-informed but the speaker seeks to create agreement on a specific course of action.

I. Attention Step.

II. Orientation Step.

III. Need Step.

IV. Satisfaction Step.

V. Summation Step.

VI. Peroration Step.

Speech to Report

This format helps you give clear, accurate information about an issue without attempting to persuade the audience to a particular perspective.

I. Attention Step.

II. Orientation Step.

A. Describe the purpose of the report.
B. Explain the background of the report.

III. Exposition Step (Explain the main points of the speech).

IV. Summation Step.

V. Peroration Step.

Speech to Explain

This format allows you to present information in such a way that the audience comprehends as many details of your subject as possible.

I. Attention Step.

II. Orientation Step.

III. Exposition Step.

IV. Summation Step.

V. Peroration Step.

Introducing Another Speaker

The purpose of an introduction is to celebrate the audience's feelings about the occasion and to bring the audience and speaker closer together. The best introducers focus on vivid incidents and experiences that raise the audience's anticipation of the speaker's information. They are spontaneous, sincere, and good humored. In addition, they are brief and to the point and careful not to steal the spotlight.

I.   The name of the speaker.

II. The speaker's accomplishments.

III. The speaker's subject.

IV. A description of the audience.

V.   A description of the occasion and how it combines the speaker, audience, and subject.

Presentation to Another Person

The purpose of a presentation is to give an award or recognition to another person. Remember that the recipient, not the presenter, should be the focus of attention. The presenter should be brief, to the point, spontaneous, sincere, and good-humored. The points in the presenter's speech should be appropriate to the occasion and the recipient's nature and character.

I.   Explain the award.

II. Celebrate the value of the award.

III. Explain the audience's part in the award.

IV. Celebrate the recipient's qualification for the award.

V.   Present the award, using the name of the recipient.

VI. If appropriate, compliment the losers for a "race well run."

Acceptance Speech

When you are offered an award, it is important to be graceful and gracious as the honor is bestowed upon you. Since you are the main attraction, act appropriately. Focus on celebrating the occasion, not yourself. As always, be brief, sincere, and good-humored.

I.   Express gratitude to the presenting group.

II. Express gratitude to those who helped you win it.

III. Express the meaningfulness of the gift itself.

IV. Accept the award on the basis of the above.

Welcome Speech

This kind of speech, quite simply, involves saying "We're glad you're here" with sincerity. Such a speech should keep in mind the benefits of the event to the participants (what they can expect to get out of it) and refrain from being deeply philosophical or serious.

I.   Introduce the occasion or person.

II. Explain the reason for the welcome.

III. Briefly explain the group's accomplishments or history.

IV. Predict the happy times to come during the occasion or because the person is there.

Speech of Goodwill

Often you will be called on to represent your organization in a positive light. The purpose of your speech will be to reinforce and develop positive attitudes toward the organization you represent. Plan your speech carefully to give a vision for your organization, describe how your organization benefits the audience, and appear pleasant but not pompous.

I.   Introduce yourself.

II. Explain in one sentence the purpose of the organization or subject you represent.

III. Explain the relationship between the organization or subject you represent and the audience.

IV. Provide one or two new facts about the organization or subject.

V.   Briefly explain the services available to the audience.

VI. Provide one example of an amazing aspect of the subject.

Eulogy

Contrary to popular belief, the eulogy is not primarily to mourn the loss of a beloved person. Rather, it is an opportunity to celebrate the memory of a person who has died and to honor the person's relationship with the audience. As a speaker, your primary concern is with the people in the audience. Attempt to phrase accurately what your audience is feeling. As you choose supporting points, think first about the effect they will have and only second about their actual importance.

I.   Reiterate the ideas your audience holds about your subject.

II. Acknowledge as appropriate the sentiments held.

III. Celebrate the peculiar relationship the subject had with the audience.

IV. Support the points you are making.

    A. The central purpose of your subject's life.

    B. The character qualities of the subject.

    C. Incidents that endeared the subject to the audience.

    D. The lesson to be learned from the life of the subject.

The Farewell Speech

The farewell is an awkward kind of speech to give. It involves "eulogizing oneself" when leaving a significant mission or position. Done properly, it communicates goodwill and keeps the lines of communication open for future relationships.

I. **Recall bright memories.**

II. **Give reasons for leaving.**

III. **Predict the future in broad terms, both for the audience and yourself.**

The Dedication Speech

It is common practice to dedicate new buildings, memorials, or organizations through a ceremonial speech. The focus of this speech should be "this _____ should inspire us to carry out the tasks which it symbolizes."

I. **Explain the reasons for the construction.**

II. **Describe the costs** (in commitment and sacrifice, not money)

III. **Honor the qualities of the builders.**

IV. **Honor the value of the object.**

V. **Describe the specific tasks the structure or institution should inspire the audience to accomplish.**

The Commencement Speech

Commencement addresses are among the most common speeches offered in America, the purpose of which is to honor the achievement of graduating students. Good commencement addresses are short, sweet and to the point.

I. **Perceive what is "truly felt" by the graduates.**

II. **Briefly acknowledge the sacrifices of those who made the graduation possible** (parents and teachers).

III. **Affirm the values or knowledge central to the institution.**

IV. **Challenge the graduates to practice the values and knowledge they have acquired.**

Bibliography

KEY QUOTE:

You now have more information and ability than 95% of the population. Just like the great communicators featured in this series, you have extraordinary gifts and opportunities.
—Jeff Myers

HOPEFULLY THE *Secrets of Great Communicators* video coaching system has spurred your growth as a communicator and sparked your interest in developing even more skills. Additional books to inspire and inform you about everything from conflict resolution to marketing your speeches include:

Resolving Conflict and Enhancing Interpersonal Relationships

The Peacemaker: A Biblical Guide to Resolving Personal Conflict by Ken Sande (Grand Rapids: Baker, 1997). Written by an attorney, this book gives practical instruction for applying biblical techniques to solve conflicts between people.

Verbal Judo: The Gentle Art of Persuasion by George J. Thompson (New York: William Morrow and Company, 1993). A consultant to police departments, the author shows clever, practical techniques for using words to disarm conflicts.

Difficult Conversations: How to Discuss What Matters Most by Douglas Stone, Bruce Patton, and Sheila Heen (New York: Penguin Books, 1999). The authors are part of the Harvard Negotiation Project, which focuses on improving communication skills in the workplace.

Strengthening Family Communication

From Playpen to Podium: How to Help Your Children Succeed in Every Area of Life by Jeff Myers (Gresham, OR: Noble, 1997). This book demonstrates how to create a stimulating communication environment in the home and develop communication skills in children from birth to age 18.

Say Goodbye to Whining, Complaining, and Bad Attitudes…In You and Your Kids! By Scott Turansky and Joanne Miller (Colorado Springs, CO: Shaw, 2000). This handy volume shows how to develop a home of honor in which positive communication can take place.

The Art of Talking With Your Teenager by Paul W. Swets (Holbrook, MA: Adams, 1995). Written by a pastor, this book shows how to open the lines of communication between parents and children.

Communication Studies as an Academic Discipline

Aristotle On Rhetoric: A Theory of Civic Discourse. Trans. George A. Kennedy (New York: Oxford, 1991). In what is considered by scholars to be the classic speech text, Aristotle catalogs and discusses speech techniques, argument strategies, and persuasion.

Lend Me Your Ears: Great Speeches in History by William Safire (New York: Norton, 1992). Written by a former political speech writer, this book contains the great speeches of history, along with insightful commentary.

Communicating for Life: Christian Stewardship in Community and Media by Quentin J. Schultze (Grand Rapids: Baker, 2000). A well-known professor of communication studies, the author fuses a biblical perspective on human communication with advice on how to communicate "Christianly."

How the News Makes Us Dumb: The Death of Wisdom in an Information Society by C. John Sommerville (Downers Grove, IL: InterVarsity, 1999). A critical look at the effects of media saturation in our lives.

Enhancing Presentation Skills

How to Hold Your Audience With Humor: A Guide to More Effective Speaking by Gene Perret (Cincinnati: Writer's Digest Books, 1984). Written by one of Bob Hope's comedy writers, this book gives tips on how to tap into your natural humor and make your speeches more entertaining.

You've Got to Be Believed to be Heard by Bert Decker (New York: St. Martin's, 1992). This highly regarded speech consultant demonstrates how to communicate effectively by reaching people at an emotional level.

Business Communication and Public Relations

Do's and Taboos Around the World by Roger E. Axtell (New York: John Wiley & Sons, 1993). Giving speeches in other countries can be difficult because of cultural barriers. This book shows what to do and what not to do as you seek to communicate cross-culturally.

Marketing With Speeches and Seminars: Your Key to More Clients and Referrals by Miriam Otte (Seattle: Zest, 1998). Giving speeches can be an excellent way to grow and promote your business. This book shows you how to do it, step by step.

Getting to Yes: Negotiating Agreement Without Giving In by Roger Fisher and William Ury (New York: Penguin Books, 1983). This short volume focuses on win-win negotiating, how to come to a negotiated agreement with integrity. Long accepted as the most important book on the subject.

Speak and Grow Rich by Dottie and Lilly Walters (New York: Prentice Hall, 1997). A helpful volume from two well-known speakers who also operate a speakers talent agency. It shows how to begin your career as a speaker, how to handle common problems, and how to grow your speaking business.

Your Public Best: The Complete Guide to Making Successful Public Appearances by Lillian Brown (New York: Newmarket, 1989). This book covers all of the essential topics to successfully presenting yourself in a positive light, including personal appearance and how to handle media interviews.

Worldview and Leadership

Thinking Like a Christian by David Noebel and Chuck Edwards (Nashville: Broadman & Holman Publishers, 2003). This worldview kit harnesses Summit Ministries' 40 years' worth of expertise in teaching worldviews—and makes it simple for you to impart to students! The kit includes an easy-to-use teacher guide, CD-ROM, video, student guide, and *Understanding the Times* reference manual.

Countering Culture: Arming Yourself to Confront Non-Biblical Worldviews by David Noebel and Chuck Edwards (Nashville: Broadman & Holman Publishers, 2004). This second book in the Worldviews in Focus series equips Christians to take a reasoned stand for biblical principles and to confront opposing worldviews in the classroom as well as in the boardroom. The complete set of materials includes a student text, an easy-to-use teacher guide on CD-ROM, and 12 video lessons.

Secrets of Everyday Leaders by Jeff Myers (Nashville: Broadman & Holman Publishers, 2005). Make a difference in the part of the world over which you have influence. Mastering good leadership skills can help you make your home, business, school, or church a more God-honoring place. *Secrets of Everyday Leaders* includes 12 video coaching sessions—6 on basic skills and 6 for more advanced training—that show you how to hone the leader in you. Featuring Dr. Jeff Myers.

Secrets of World Changers by Jeff Myers (Nashville: Broadman & Holman Publishers, 2006). Find an exciting sense of direction with this biblical approach to gaining a vision, unleashing your God-given gifts, renewing your motivation, and achieving your highest goals. This ground-breaking approach to leadership shows how God can use your gifts, however humble, to have an extraordinary influence on the world.

For a complete listing of resources offered by the Myers Institute, go to www.myersinstitute.com.